THE MEN IN BLACK

If nc

2

THE MEN IN BLACK

Tony O'Neill

with Peter Walsh

MILO BOOKS

First published in hardback in October 2005
by Milo Books
This paperback edition published in June 2006

ISBN 978-1-9038-5452-5

Typeset by Avon DataSet Ltd,
Bidford on Avon, Warwickshire, B50 4JH

Printed in Great Britain by
Cox & Wyman Ltd, Reading

MILO BOOKS LTD
The Old Weighbridge
Station Road
Wrea Green
Lancs PR4 2PH
www.milobooks.com

Contents

Preface   vii

1   Target Kilo   1
2   Operation Mars   23
3   Busted   42
4   Welcome to Hell   65
5   Football Intelligence   77
6   Contenders   91
7   Gangchester United   101
8   Slashed   120
9   The Night of the Balaclavas   127
10 Hooligans Abroad   141
11 The Men In Black   155
12 Awaydays   172
13 Superfirm   194
14 Old Habits Die Hard   207
15 The Final Whistle   234

PREFACE

'Hi Pete. It's Debbie. Have you heard about Tony?'

'No.'

'He's been shot.'

Shot?

'Is he alright?'

'Well, he's in the MRI, on the high dependency wing. He's had surgery but he's fine at the moment.'

In a week's time, I was due to publish Tony O'Neill's first book, *Red Army General*, the partial story of his life as the leading Manchester United football hooligan. I was accustomed to last-minute glitches with books – a delay at the printers, an error spotted in a caption – but taking a phone call from an author's wife to say he had taken a bullet at the weekend and was in intensive care was not one of them.

I also knew, however, that it wasn't the first time. Eleven years earlier, Tony had been blasted with a sawn-off shotgun at a Manchester nightclub. On that occasion he had contracted septicaemia and almost died. This time his injuries didn't seem so bad – or so I thought.

A few days later, I went to visit him in Manchester Royal

Infirmary. He lay on a bed near the entrance to the ward, a mess of tubes and monitors, with Debbie sitting beside him. A long, grisly seam of stitches stretched the length of his sternum. Never one for a suntan, he looked pale as death.

I had brought along a number of his freshly-printed books. We had promised some people signed copies, and this was my first chance to get him to autograph them. Tony gleefully seized on this as evidence of my mercenary approach: as he lay gravely ill in hospital, his publisher cared only about selling books. It was the kind of hard-hearted behaviour he secretly approved of.

'Here he is,' he growled in gruff Mancunian as I walked in. 'I'm lying here dying and all he can think about is getting his books sold. Fucking ruthless.'

Oh well, I thought, *at least I've cheered him up.*

I had first met Tony 'Buckethead' O'Neill in HMP Sudbury, off the A50 between Stoke and Derby. He was serving a sentence for violent disorder before an England international match in Manchester. The prosecution had alleged that he led a group into a pub to fight some rival hooligans from another city. He denied it, the jury didn't believe him, and the judge jailed him for three years and nine months.

Sudbury is an open prison and Bucket had wangled a job in the officers' canteen. So we sat down there, with tables of lunching prison warders a few yards away, to discuss plans for a book about his life.

Bucket was almost unique in having been involved on the front line of football hooliganism in four separate decades, from the very early Seventies through to the early Noughties. Police had marked him out as the ringleader of United's 'firm' during an undercover investigation in the late Eighties, and ever since then he had been one of their core targets. Latterly he had run trips to United games at home and abroad through his travel company, Champions Sports Travel, based in a

sparsely-furnished office a stone's throw from Old
His name, and nickname, were legendary in Man
football circles and beyond.

No United hooligan had every written a memoir, despite the
growing ubiquity of the genre. Tony was the best man to do it,
but would probably never have done so had he not been given
such a long sentence for what he considered a minor event in
which no-one was hurt. He felt bitter about it, but also knew the
hooligan heyday was over. Perhaps it was his way of drawing a
line.

He worked on the manuscript in prison, and then over the
next few months during his release on licence. His personality
and character emerged through the pages, as well as in our
regular meetings and discussions.

It wasn't hard to see why he was a leader. Tall and physically
imposing, he had a forceful personality and a direct manner.
Bucket's bark was the equal of his bite. It would be fair to say he
is a man of strong opinions, which he is not afraid to voice,
sometimes loudly.

But I came to realise the method in his outbursts. Sometimes
they disguised what he was really thinking; while you were
listening to him, he was weighing you up and judging your
responses. He was as streetwise as an alley cat, and if he didn't
want to discuss something, would simply change the subject,
and that was the end of that.

We decided on two books, the first ending around 1987, the
second beginning with the origins of the undercover Operation
Mars and going up to 2005. The first was duly finished, and
once the publicity was out of the way, we were due to start the
second, *The Men In Black*.

Then came the shooting, the details of which are still murky
and may never be publicly disclosed. He was released from
hospital relatively quickly, though his injuries were serious: the

bullet had pierced his colon and liver and irreparably damaged nerves in his back. After a short spell at home he was rushed back to hospital in agony, with his internal injuries bleeding.

Again he recovered, but over the next few months it became apparent how ill he was. Tony is not someone who readily shows weakness, but a diet of pain-numbing morphine tablets seemed to effect not just on his energy but his personality. He hit a low, and was only pulled back up, oddly enough, when he visited an acupuncturist, whose mysterious, ancient methods restored some imbalance in his body and made the painkillers redundant.

Now he's back at his desk at his Champion Sports Travel office, wheeling and dealing with his unique telephone manner, the only man who can make the word 'Hello' sound like a challenge and an inquisition at the same time. His attitude to everything that has happened to him is summed up in his fatalistic motto: Whatever happens, happens. You pick yourself up, dust yourself down and throw yourself back into the fray. That's how he was in a mass brawl, that's how he is in life.

Other people have contributed to this book, from opposite ends of the hooligan scale. Steve Barnes was a Greater Manchester Police football intelligence officer during a period of intense activity by United's 'Men in Black'. He eventually had to leave the force after the discovery of a near-fatal brain tumour, and kindly consented to giving us his recollections of the men he targeted for the best part of a decade, and how he did it. Paul Doyle, on the other hand, was by his own admission a gangster, some say *the* gangster, in the most gang-ridden city in England. Football violence to him was merely a recreational release from the rigours of an even more dangerous line of work.

They exemplify the broad spectrum of people attracted by the excitement, the so-called buzz, of soccer violence. Of course, the Tony O'Neill story is not to many tastes. Most people despise hooliganism (though some just *profess* to despise it) and see no merit in fighting purely for the hell of it, even if both sides are willing.

What many cannot deny, though, is that they find the Tony O'Neills of this world to be intriguing characters, who have led extraordinary lives and have seen and done things beyond the scope – or inclination – of most men their age.

The era of the British hooligan is passing, and few will mourn its demise. But it happened. This is the story of some of those in the thick of it.

Peter Walsh, October 2005

Chapter One

TARGET KILO

THREE EXTRAORDINARY MONTHS in 1985 marked a watershed in modern football hooliganism. On March 13, scenes of Millwall fans rioting inside Luton Town's Kenilworth Road ground and chasing police across the pitch were watched on television by, among others, a horrified Prime Minister, Margaret Thatcher. Two months later, on May 11, yobs from Birmingham City and Leeds United staged an even more violent riot at St Andrew's, and a young fan died when a wall collapsed after the game; the events were overshadowed, however, by the deaths of fifty-six people in a fire at Bradford City's Valley Parade ground on the same day. Then, on May 29, the storming of a segregation fence by Liverpool supporters led to panic and a crowd surge that resulted in the deaths of thirty-nine spectators at the European Cup final between Liverpool and Juventus at the Heysel Stadium in Belgium.

Something had to be done, and quickly. Clearly the safety of many football stadia was inadequate. Just as importantly, the tide of violence that had been growing ever since the appearance of the 'casual' gangs at the start of the decade had to be halted. The Football Association's first response, post-Heysel, was to ban English clubs from playing in Europe. Then the Government weighed in. 'We have to get the game cleaned up from this hooliganism and then perhaps we shall be able to go overseas again,' said Margaret Thatcher. The central plank of her response was a bill introducing, among other measures, compulsory computerised membership schemes at clubs (though this would eventually fall foul of Lord Justice Taylor's Report after the Hillsborough Disaster, and be quietly shelved). More severe sentences signalled a clampdown by the courts too.

Perhaps the most important reaction, however, was at first unseen. A number of British police forces decided to infiltrate the soccer gangs using undercover officers. These specially trained officers would pose as fans, even as hooligans, to gather evidence against the ringleaders and their followers. It was a big financial investment and a new departure for many forces, involving methods more typically used to make controlled buys from drug dealers. Up to that time, only British Transport Police could be considered especially knowledgeable about hooligan gangs, largely because of the problems they had faced on the rail network over two decades. Most urban police forces had little or no intelligence on the hardcore hooligans at their clubs.

Manchester United, despite the size of the club and its following, was not initially a target. In the Seventies, United's Red Army had become infamous, its exploits a byword for hooliganism around the world. But by the Eighties, others gangs had surpassed United's mob, in notoriety at least. Four 'firms' in particular – the West Ham Inter-City Firm, the Chelsea Headhunters, the Millwall Bushwhackers and the Leeds Service Crew – became especially infamous in what is often seen as the heyday of hooliganism. All four served time in the Second Division, where the opportunity for disorder at smaller grounds, with fewer police, was greater. All had evocative and recognisable gang names, while United didn't. And some of their leaders were becoming increasingly high-profile; in August 1985, for instance, a Thames Television documentary entitled *Hooligan* followed members of the ICF around the country, including a lively trip to Old Trafford.

Big-spending United remained in the top division, occasional cup winners and perennial title challengers. In 1986 they had employed a new manager, Alex Ferguson, who with Aberdeen had broken the Old Firm's lock on Scottish football. His stewardship did not begin well. Off the pitch, United still had possibly the biggest hooligan mob around. In fact it was more than one mob, with various groups split by age. The Cockney Reds always formed a large part of United's mob.

Chelsea, Birmingham City, West Ham, Millwall, Crystal Palace, Leeds, Luton and Wolverhampton Wanderers were all targets between March 1986 and April 1988, in operations with names like Own Goal, Wild Boar, Spoonbill and Red Card. Interestingly, only Chelsea and Luton were in the First Division at the time. The trend was replicated in Manchester, where police targeted not United but their great rivals City, then in the Second Division. Often in the shadow of United, both on and off the pitch, City's more violent element had been making waves in the lower division. Their younger element, the Young Guvnors or Governors, were particularly active.

In 1987, Greater Manchester Police formed the Omega Squad to infiltrate the Guvnors and the Young Guvnors. Highly trained and secretive, the Omega Squad's remit was potentially dangerous undercover work. Young officers were selected and trained to adopt false identities and to think on their feet while working in the field. It would later grow to tackle drug dealers, armed robbers and other serious criminals, but in its original incarnation it targeted the hooligans of City and United, with officers alternating between the matches of each in an attempt to find out who was who and what was going on. It was not, at that stage, a 'football intelligence' (FI) operation – in keeping with other forces, GMP did not have specialist FI officers at that time, although it did have football liaison officers, who worked with the clubs to organise match-day policing and other matters.

It was at Maine Road that the work of Omega first bore fruit. After seven months of following the gangs and trying to win their confidence – with one officer sometimes taking lads to games in his van – police raided the homes of members of the Guvnors and Young Guvnors in February 1988. Twenty-six would eventually be charged, most with conspiracy to commit riot, or violent disorder.

Shortly after their arrest, a British Transport policeman suffered a fractured skull at Piccadilly Station when he tried to stop a firm of Young Guvnors attacking United fans returning from Arsenal. Then in May 1988, police filmed a fight on Chester Road, Old Trafford, between young United fans and a mob of Young Guvnors at United full-back Arthur Albiston's testimonial. One youth was kicked and stamped on while prone on the floor. Though many of those involved both in the original Operation Omega arrests and in the two subsequent incidents were later jailed, clearly the problem of soccer gang warfare in Manchester had not been solved.

In August 1988, GMP formed a football intelligence desk as part of its general Force Criminal Intelligence office. A sergeant, Stephen Fox, was tasked with gathering information and producing bulletins to notify local officers of 'active and potential troublemakers'. His remit covered all the Football League grounds in the Greater Manchester Police area, including United, City, Bolton Wanderers, Oldham Athletic, Stockport County, Rochdale, Bury and Wigan Athletic.

One United hooligan – Tony O'Neill – was brought to the

notice of the desk immediately: firstly, by the M Division football intelligence officer at Stretford, who was responsible for Old Trafford and who reported that O'Neill had been involved in minor football-related matters; and secondly, by the British Transport Police at Piccadilly Station, who said they had dealt with O'Neill in 1985 for 'unlawful use of railway tickets'. Sgt Fox would later note: 'Whilst O'Neill's criminal record did not specifically relate to any involvement in organised football violence, he was known to be of a violent disposition, to follow Manchester United both home and away, and was believed to be involved in organising transport to away fixtures.' However, Sgt Fox did not at that time have a photograph of O'Neill, and had never seen him.

Indeed their intelligence in the early days was poor. They did not even know that O'Neill had recently served a four-month jail term after being arrested after a match at Tottenham in 1986. But it was clear that United's large hooligan element had not gone away.

In January 1989, one of the heavyweight mobs of the hooligan world visited Old Trafford. A United lad later recalled what happened in the fanzine *Red Issue*.

RED ISSUE: Millwall had gone about spanking United at the Den in the Seventies. They didn't do anything of note at Old Trafford, and at that time they weren't particularly well known. All people really knew about them is they were a tight-knit, clannish lot from a particularly rough part of South East London and so the districts they drew their support from were rough. Lads old enough to remember relayed the tale of the trip to the Den in Division Two. It's true, the United fans actually there that night did get terrorised.

United's main special never arrived though, as a pea-souper halted the train somewhere round Milton Keynes. It arrived that late at Euston that the police just turned it round and sent it straight back to Manchester. That's not to deny the truth of Millwall's claims, merely to point out that things could have been very different. They certainly didn't have the numbers then that they had in later years, i.e. the mid-to-late Eighties. So 1989 then, and a lot had been said about this one in advance. People just couldn't wait for it to come round. We'd waited fifteen years to set the record straight.

Millwall, give them their due, were just as keen. To my knowledge, at this point, only Glasgow Rangers had ever come in our end wholesale and blatantly advertised the fact, at a friendly in '74. Sunderland had turned up in the League Cup in '76, not to have a go, just to watch the game but they neglected to come in disguise. They chose the Scoreboard Paddock, presumably thinking that as it was opposite the Stretford End, it wouldn't be so partisan. Big mistake. The equivalent of away fans in Liverpool saying, we won't go on the Kop, we'll go on the Annie Road instead. They got done in all over, chased off the paddock, across the corner of the pitch past the Old Trafford Paddock and up to the old players tunnel. There they got leathered to such a degree it took the police fifteen minutes to restore order. The OB were even quoted after as saying something like 'could they have just not bothered and saved everyone the trouble?' So whilst all sorts of fans of other clubs have sneaked in over the years, none have had the guts to accept our firm's invitation to take a section of OT, let alone advertise the fact in advance.

Liverpool, Chelsea, West Ham, Everton, none of them ever took up the option. The patchy (by our standards) attendances of the Eighties meant there were always big blocks of tickets available. The scope was there but no-one was up to the challenge. Until Millwall. You've got to give them their due, they knew no one had done it and they wanted to outdo all the supposedly top Cockney firms and be the first. Sure, Leeds had looked the part in '81, but they definitely didn't live up to expectations.

Moving on to '89 then and ticket touting was big business at OT, even then. It was better in some ways than it is now, as you'd pick up cheap spares from various sources and on the day sell them to people queuing at the cash turnstiles at face value.

Millwall were making a big show of their top-flight status. They were trying to do everything big time. We'd heard stories about them chartering flights to games in the North West, and for the game at OT, two hundred of them rolled up as a firm at Ringway. They were joined by another hundred on coaches. Given the grafts that people from lots of the big service crews of the Eighties had tumbled over the years, it was unsurprising that the ticket spiv network stretched all over the country. Through Cockney contacts word was received from Millwall. 'We want three hundred tickets in a section of your ground. We're going to come in and do a proper job, we know no-one else has done it, so we're going to be the first.' Remember, our previous accolade was the first West Ham firm that made a brief visit to the United Road in '82. Millwall were intent on outdoing anything anyone else had ever done. You have to respect their ambition.

Upsetting as it might be for any club official to read this, it didn't take two minutes for five Manchester touts to acquire 300 tickets for B stand which were promptly served up to one Cockney tout with a nice earner built in. This was all set up a good three weeks in advance. On the day, the two hundred on the charter flight took a train from the airport into town and went to try and make a show. There, the police had things well under control and they were rounded up and escorted in short order. The late Eighties were almost as bad as the Nineties for days out with the dibble.

I don't know if they had any of those late-Eighties mobile

phones but they timed it just right. The two coaches arrived concurrently with the escort and were allowed to park next to the old souvenir shop on the forecourt. Millwall were clever and mingled through their shirt wearers at the away turnstiles and drifted across to go in B stand in threes and fours.

The area was thick with our lads, but everyone was focussed on the main event and there was no off in prospect on the forecourt. Some of the kids off the buses even shouted that they were part of the mob going in B stand and that they'd see us inside. Indeed they would. Some of us drifted through them on our way to our own sections in the South Stand. Others even took the long way round down United Road and round the back of the Stretford End, so it wasn't obvious we were all diving in the Main Stand for the first time in our lives. The majority of the lads had done something unheard of and got in the ground for half two. Only the last few hundred went in late.

Millwall came in, and give them credit, they did look the part. They didn't look frightened and there was a definite intent about them. As they were moving to their seats the Old Trafford Paddock at the bottom started chanting at them.

Everyone knew they were coming of course and had done for about a fortnight. It had taken precisely 4.2 nanoseconds for that news to go round town. Once the barmies at the bottom had started up, the attention of the whole ground was put right on these Millwall. The firm was intent on waiting for a goal or a serious foul to kick it off but in no time at all the kids in the OT Paddock spilled out onto the track and charged across the front of the Main Stand, intent on getting to grips with the invaders.

The time for tactics had passed then but our strategic placement would prove more than adequate. As one, the firm occupying A stand was up and into the back of them. More were positioned on Millwall's left as they gazed at the barmies demonstrating beneath them. Their main tactical error though, had been not buying up all the B stand so there was also a small team on their immediate right. They were hit then from three sides whilst their attention was focussed on the fourth, and that's never a good starting point for a fight. We must have had six or seven hundred all told. Even C and D stands were full of thugs and they had to charge across the front of the directors' box to get involved. I'll never forget Martin Edwards' moral outrage afterwards. 'It was just a sea of animals. It was an absolute disgrace. We had guests from Millwall in that section and thugs were charging en masse, etc.'

They didn't even stop the game as a thousand lads battled in the Main Stand. It went on hell for leather. The ferocity of our lads was frightening. Millwall were game, but their resistance didn't last a minute. They were totally overwhelmed and swept away. They were outnumbered to be fair but we were that revved up to prove this was a move you absolutely did not make. Millwall were bowled over seats and massacred. We wanted to rubber-stamp no-one else ever being foolhardy enough to try this ever again. It was awesome. The only thing that surprises me about it all is no-one ended up down in the paddock, though one sight of the barmies in there surging up and down the terrace inviting the cockneys to join them would have given even the most desperate fugitive pause for thought. Some even tried to climb up to get at them. The directors box had been abandoned, the Main Stand's in uproar and in front there's just a seething mass. Somewhere in all that there were twenty-two blokes kicking a ball around.

You only got two minutes with people by this stage though, so they had a minute's attempt at resistance and a minute of getting slapped before the police came in. They had a simple plan of forcing the Cockneys down the stairs onto the concourse at the back of the B stand. That didn't work too well, as we all piled down the adjacent stair wells and had it with them again downstairs. The fighting downstairs was all the fiercer in the confined space, I mean truly violent. All veneer of civilisation had gone, we were back in the Stone Age and happy for it. The OB took the unprecedented step of opening the main gates to let them out of the ground before someone died. In the midst of all this, a Millwall fan got stabbed in the arse, as one of his mates would relate to me later in life. 'We couldn't believe it, stabbed in that day and age. In the ground too, it was fucking unheard of.'

The dibble took Millwall round and shoved them in the away section, though some stragglers might have remained penned in A [stand], I can't remember. They must have wondered why on earth they'd bothered. They could have turned up, made a decent showing and gone in their own section, but no, they had to be big time and they paid the price.

After the game, and as was the style of the time, the police had everything well under control. They kept Millwall in for ages whilst a mixed firm of us and barmies numbering perhaps 2,000 waited outside. Those on the coaches were slung on and escorted out of town no problem. Those catching a train . . . weren't put on at the ground, as by this time the police knew we'd be up the tracks waiting for them. Instead, they marched them down to Old Trafford station having cleared that, and locked down all stations in between. It had resolved down to perhaps two hundred each outside the station and Millwall did put on a bit of a charge in an attempt to save face. There was a little contact as they made the point that they don't give in. We even had a bit of a go with the police, which was quite something in 1989 but the OB had it all sorted in the end, and that was that.

Games like Millwall at home indicated to GMP that the problem of thuggery was perhaps as bad as ever. They needed to get a handle on it, and to do that they had to find out who was behind it. The new football intelligence desk began slowly to collate information on some of United's more active and influential hooligans, but would receive no further substantiated intelligence on the main man, Tony O'Neill, until he was arrested after a match against Nottingham Forest on March 18, 1989. Forest had brought a firm to Old Trafford and the Manchester lads turned out in force to have a crack at them.

TONY: It was a cup game at Old Trafford and we lost 1–0. Forest came into town early and everyone was onto them, running around town like lunatics. We couldn't really get at them because of the police. Next thing, I'm in the ground and there's chaos – a dispute over a goal and everyone is going mad. After the game we go round to their end. They used to keep them in but the inspector who was in charge at the ground had only been on for two weeks and didn't know what he was doing. He decided that because we both wore red and white, he would let the fans out together and they would mingle happily.

Fair play to Forest, their boys tried to come out, but the forecourt was swamped with United going at the gates. Forest got done in and forced back in a couple of times, but they didn't stay there; they eventually tried to come up Warwick Road as a mob, not just their firm but their whole crowd, and I hadn't seen that before. It was fantastic. They were always going to get pummelled but they went for it.

The police tried to control it but couldn't. For five minutes Forest got hit from every side but were trying to have a go back. As they were bounced from side to side, their mob slowly disintegrated. By the time they got to the top of Warwick Road there was only about fifteen or twenty of them left as a tight firm, with a few coppers trying to protect them. The copper at the front who stopped the traffic also stopped the rest of the crowd, and so this scraggly little bunch got across the road outside the Trafford pub. The Forest that had scattered now had a focal point to regroup around and jumped back in to join up again. Then they got the big police escort all the way back to Piccadilly.

Once Chester Road had calmed down, we walked along heading to town. My mistake was crossing the road with a small group of lads. This brought the attention of the police, who decided, now that it was quiet, 'There's the bastard.' The van pulled up and they all jumped out, led by a Sgt Johnson from Longsight police station. They arrested me and another lad, Notty. Basically they had lost the plot earlier on and now it was time to make amends and start making arrests.

I was thrown onto the floor of the van with a boot on my neck, with a bunch of police thugs for company. I did notice as I was being dragged in that there was a blue, unmarked police car just behind us. To me they were obviously football intelligence.

There were three of us in the van, including a lad I didn't know. The FI officer came to the door, pointed to this third lad and they threw him out. I was then taken to the police station and charged with fighting in the street, when there was actually no fighting at the time I was arrested.

The police had their story and I had mine. The date eventually arrives at Trafford Magistrates Court and I'm defending myself. I have read their story: four coppers against me. Notty should have been with me but his solicitor decided no way did he want his client to be in a trial with me defending myself, so they went for a separate trial. She thought I was off my head representing myself and her client would get dragged down by me, but she didn't have a clue.

I knew I was up against a pack of lies and would have to

combat them. I got my own witnesses. Allegedly there's a group of professional witnesses on tour, ringers who will turn out for the defence if the price is right. I wouldn't know about that, but I do know that for two days the police spewed out their rubbish but failed to mention the football intelligence officer turning up at the van. This was their downfall. I questioned them for two days, and my own witnesses for two days. I was put in the dock myself and slaughtered the prosecutor. He couldn't budge me or any of my witnesses and the only people who looked sheepish were the police because they were tripping up over their story.

It became clear to the court that I had been targeted and that the officers had known who I was, even though they denied it and kept referring to me in court as 'a man who I now know to be Tony O'Neill.' After several days, I was found not guilty. We are laughing and jumping up and down. The prosecutor comes over, sticks his hand out, shakes my hand, congratulates me, and then had the cheek to say, 'What really happened?'

'The cops lied through their teeth and made you look an idiot,' I said.

'Well, we're all Reds anyway,' he said. Turns out he was a United fan too.

That case gave me a great feeling, not only to win but to do it representing myself and to see the faces of the coppers, ill because they have been done by a thug.

On leaving Trafford Mags, I went straight to Olliers solicitors and explained what had gone on. I told them who I was and that I was being targeted and wanted to take out civil proceedings for unlawful arrest, malicious prosecution and false imprisonment. I got legal aid for it, and sued the Chief Constable of Greater Manchester Police.

It took *nine* years to get to court – and lo and behold, they bring up the football intelligence officer who I said was there pointing out people. He starts to read from some document describing my activities but does not produce one ounce of proof. The other officers stand up in court and all they can keep saying is, 'I can't remember, it was nine years ago.' From me having a sound case, the delay of nine years has scuppered it because now they're all saying, 'I'm only reading from my notes, I can't remember.' But they then have a full defence team using FI against me which they had previously denied.

To cut a long story short, I lost the case. From looking good to get a few quid compensation, I'm given another kick in the bollocks, although this time not literally. I couldn't believe it: I had my witnesses, it was all boxed off, sewn up and bang to rights, and the system fucked us. Reading between the lines, they had lifted me that day because they wanted me to have a football violence conviction; they were getting ready to arrest us all in Operation Mars and a recent violence conviction against me would have strengthened their case no end.

Funnily enough, when I first sued them for wrongful arrest, in June 1990, I wrote in my deposition: 'I am not paranoid about the police, rather I am convinced that I am the victim of a police campaign against me. There is a lot of media attention on the subject of football hooliganism and this is something that has gone on for some years. There have been a number of large scale trials, for example at Chelsea, West Ham and more recently at Manchester City. It would not surprise me in the least if I was arrested early one morning as part of a dawn police raid involving many officers and many arrests. I can imagine a police case being built around alleged football hooliganism at Manchester United and I would envisage myself being charged for conspiring to commit public order offences at football grounds. The situation would be that I would be regarded as some kind of "general".'

Now I'm not claiming I can see into the future, but four months later that's exactly what happened [see Chapter 3].

On May 27, 1989, two months after Tony's arrest at the Forest game, Sgt Fox and a detective constable travelled up to Hampden Park in Glasgow to act as spotters at a Scotland v England international. While there, they followed groups of fans, tried to identify known faces, and took rolls and rolls of film. Due to other work pressures, however, they would not get around to reviewing the negatives until five months later. When they did, they saw Tony O'Neill with a group involved in fighting outside the ground.

TONY: The England scene has never been one that got me going, for one reason: being a United fanatic, the passion for my team consumed everything in me. No way could I get passionate about watching anyone else, not even my national team. United has consumed my life, so trying to watch and sing along with any other fans does nothing for me. All my excitement is with United, from getting up in the morning on a match day to going to bed. I still can't get my head round how people can switch, you support your team from childhood until death, that's how it should be.

With England you get a lot of followers from smaller clubs who are looking to big themselves up to the cameras and say hello to other groups, thus avoiding contact when you play each other, as they all start claiming to be friends. Plus the political side, 'Rule Britannia' and all that, lads portraying themselves as loyal to Queen and country, no surrender to the IRA and all this mix with the Orangemen. I'm sorry but to me your team is your life, not some left-wing, right-wing, fascist, revolutionary Bolshevik, money-making, whatever-they-call-themselves, idealists. For fuck's sake, where's your brain?

The England scene was great back in the Seventies, Eighties

15

and very early Nineties for the hoolies. The lads from United used to go regularly and they had some great tales to tell, lots of shoplifting and thieving, fighting the Germans, the Dutch, etc. Other gangs were there like the Scousers and Cockneys but not till after the Seventies, as they couldn't get it together. The Cockneys couldn't even get it together for the Scots in their own London Town until segregation with tickets was introduced. I might be wrong about them not travelling much with England in the Seventies but my recollection is that it was mainly lads from the North West, so please don't get on your keypads down south, it's only my recollection.

I have watched England only four or five times and that started in Glasgow in 1989. Six o'clock, Manchester Piccadilly, and there's about sixty of us and a few more when we arrive, totalling about 120. The train reaches the city at 10:30 and we're expecting a load of Jocks to be waiting, but there's nothing, which considering all the talk was a letdown. There were no marauding gangs of English back then, no Birmingham wanting to fight Wolves in Glasgow or Boro looking for Newcastle, and the reason was there was no police protection then like there is now, no-one to hide behind if it came on top.

We realised that sooner rather than later this place was going to be filled with mad Jocks and they would be on us, so we made our way through the town, stopping twice to have a quick pint before we settled into a pub a mile from the ground. Unbeknown to us, the road we were on was one of the main routes to the ground, and when we vacated the place, with one or two fruit machines and the cigarette machine empty, the road was full of Jocks dressed from head to toe in tartan.

Walking along this road to the ground and all tight together we looked a sight, as none of us wore colours and so all the Jocks knew exactly what we were: football hoolies. The Jocks were singing, dancing and pissed up and on seeing us they came over and started doing their tribal war chants of Scotland this and how they hate the English. Incredibly, they actually seemed shocked and surprised when they were put on their arses. Did they really think they could act up without a response? Well, quite a few ended up on the floor.

We came to the top of the road and the police were now there with horses. As we approached and could see loads of Jocks standing about, all hell let loose. The Jocks hurled everything in their hands at us, filling the air. We were dodging cans, bottles, bricks, lumps of wood, the lot. We ran around the horses to the nearest Jocks and got stuck into them. It was chaos, with coppers coming off horses, Jocks on the floor, a proper scrap. It was good fun as it was more of a disturbance than vicious and it lasted for a few minutes until we got through with the help of police horses that didn't care who they trampled.

That day only some of us managed to get in the ground but enough in case anybody wanted to have a pop at us. But nothing happened of note. We were kept in after the game and came out to find the rest of the lads waiting outside. The police marched several hundred back to town and as we got to the edge of town there was a mob on a corner. We soon recognised some of Notts Forest's lads, so we got out of the escort, which was disintegrating anyway as people were going in different directions. We quickly got together and came round the corner where they were stood hanging about on the pavement and around some buses. Not for long. The first punch landed and the cry of 'United!' went up. They didn't stand a chance because they didn't see it coming. We scattered them all over the streets.

We split up and arranged to meet in an hour so we wouldn't bring the police down on us. Eventually we settled down in a pub for the night's entertainment, only interrupted by some scruffy cunts who claimed to be Aberdeen but soon fucked off.

Our train was due to go but we said, fuck it. We had enjoyed ourselves so much that we were happy to hit the station at pub closing time and catch whatever train was in when we got there. It was the 11:30 p.m. train stopping at Preston, Crewe and London, so we got on, joined by Manchester's finest British Transport police, who had been waiting for us to go home and knew we'd eventually turn up. We knew they would just want to get us home and they duly obliged by getting the train diverted to Manchester. Who can blame them, as no one would have appreciated receiving us lot in some small town in the early hours; a few wise lads might well have got their day's money back with a few illegal methods.

It had been a great day out but the match and atmosphere were lousy, as they so often are at England games. Who wants to listen to all that political chanting and see all those Hitler salutes for the benefit of the cameras? Fuckwits, the lot of 'em.

———

Sgt Fox had received a photo of Tony after his arrest at the Forest game. He first saw and recognised Tony himself while conducting pre-match observations at the United v Millwall game on September 16, 1989. Coincidentally, this was the first match at which O'Neill noticed the police filming United's lads after the game, from the safety of their blue riot vans. At the start of that season, Sgt Fox had introduced a system of targeting individuals by sending intelligence bulletins to Tactical Aid Group patrols on match days. The dreaded TAG were GMP's shock troops, public disorder specialists who could beat any hooligan mob at their own game.

If the police needed any convincing to investigate United's mob, it came on 23 September 1989, at Maine Road. City were newly promoted to what was then the Barclays First Division, and so it was the first time the two Manchester giants had met in the league for two and half years. The match would end in a 5–1 win for City but was marred throughout by mass fighting inside and outside the ground, with 200 United yobs infiltrating City's North Stand.

TONY: The Grey Parrot pub in Hulme was run by my pal, who used to be a City fan but changed for the better. It was a large pub in the middle of what you would describe as a shithole but believe me, up to 1,000 people, mainly lads, would plot up there sometimes. A twelve o'clock kick-off didn't matter to us, as we would have the doors open at 7 a.m. and often by nine o'clock you couldn't get in, so the large car park became the outside office.

One such occasion was in September 1989, when we decided we were going in the North Stand at Maine Road. This was no small occasion; it was the big one, the first time we'd met City in a league game for several years. Everyone was told, 'Don't buy any ticket unless it is for the North Stand.' We had a little help from one of the best spivs about, who was a Man City lad, so their mob certainly knew what we were up to. We were coming and we were going to cause havoc all day and all night.

The only problem was the police, who were in and around Hulme waiting for the eventful march to Maine Road. More than 1,000 people were drinking in and outside the Grey Parrot and many were pissed out of their heads, as they had been there from seven or eight in the morning. This recipe of pissed-up lads and sober heads is ideal for a riot. It no longer mattered how the police tried to control this group, they were bound to fail.

As we neared the ground, large groups began to break off and run down side streets, pursued by police. It didn't matter, as we were always going to get to the North Stand. The only problem was if there would be a reception committee waiting for the first few to get in. Having been helped by one of their lads to get our tickets and so infiltrate their section, we were fully expecting a massive reception committee. The mad scramble was on as United were coming round corners, out of alleyways, and getting together to go through the turnstiles. The police were baffled but in we went.

No reception committee. Everyone made their way to a section of the ground behind the goal, where they knew to congregate. We had all been there for a while, and City were doing nothing, no charging or wanting to come down and have it toe to toe, they were overwhelmed.

The game started and then the fun began. A few punches were traded and things began to fly in our direction. The lads start going into City fans who are giving it large and the whole area erupts. City fans are coming from all over but not coming into the main firm, who are standing together. The whole scene is utter chaos all around us as people are trapped under seats and falling at the front. There is no escape for both sides as high fencing stops people slipping away from the trouble. People from both sides who want to get out can't. Fists are flying all around and the police are trying to stop it but there's too many people. We're still in the middle holding the area, with a gap all around us which City will not come into. We are aware of our vulnerable position but not from the Blues, from the cameras filming us, so because of this we all stay together and there's no further charging around from us. But close to the fence it's mayhem, which only stops once the game has been stopped and the players are taken off for eight minutes because of the violence.

There's now fans spilling through a gate onto the pitch side and all around it there's punches coming both ways as the City fans are throwing cheap punches on people who are clearly on the way out. I've heard many stories of United and City fans punching each other in the chaos, which lasted about fifteen minutes. About 200 of us were left in the ground and all sat down with a gap around us. The police threw out a few but in the main a nice firm was still present up until half-time.

On the whistle of half-time, one of our chaps, Wing, led most of the lads under the stand and the police were waiting: they opened the exit doors and kicked them out with their own version of politeness. This now looked bad for those of us left, but throughout the second half there were no problems. We all knew the show would start at the end.

I made my way out five minutes early, only to be met by a few hundred United charging in the direction I had just come from. So off we all went, back for a fight. We were unable to get past the line of horses and cops to get back in but City's lads appeared in small groups at the corner of the Kippax and North Stand. Into them we went, chasing them back in the Kippax – which was nice, as it had been a while since United had been in there. The fight grew as more and more of us piled through the gate, forcing City back to the corner stairway. It wasn't one-way traffic but we were on top and all loving it.

The mounted police were now the ones to avoid and they were swinging their horses around into us to disperse the mob. One thing you don't argue with in that situation is a fucking big horse, as there's going to be broken bones, so eventually we were out of there and charging around the side streets, which were now a scene of utter madness. People were being knocked out everywhere you looked.

We ended up outside the City Social Club, where many United had already gathered. Claremont Road now witnessed 5–600 of United's lads giving it to any City who came at us. We were fighting the full length of the road and no one could stop us. Eventually we hit Princess Parkway, with City nowhere. We had fucked them off. We headed back to our pub in Hulme and there was no chance of City coming there – they never did. Funny that, considering it's supposed to be 'their' area.

THE MEN IN BLACK

———

The trouble was described as the worst at a Manchester football ground for years. 'They were fighting like dogs in the Kippax, the Main Stand and the back of the North Stand,' said Chief Superintendent Ray Sherratt. 'When we saw the trouble begin in the front area, which had been infiltrated by United supporters, my men were already calling for back up in other sections.' Thirty-nine fans were ejected from the ground and twenty-six arrested.

City could claim that their mob had been depleted by the Operation Omega arrests, and for United that match perhaps marked the start of something similar. Operation Mars was about to begin. Using the experience gained in Operation Omega, the undercover squad would now try to do the same with United's mob. It would quickly identify a leader of the United fans, a man who more than any other the police were determined to bring to book: Tony O'Neill, who they codenamed Target Kilo.

Chapter Two

OPERATION MARS

THE OFFICIAL OPERATION Mars observation logs began on 9 December 1989, at a home game against Crystal Palace. Four officers, identified only as Derek M., John O., Paul G. and Paul D., visited several Manchester pubs, including Merchants Wine Bar and the Kings in Oldham Street, and the Dog and Partridge near the stadium in Old Trafford, and recorded what they saw. Little of note happened apart from some 'obscene and threatening chants . . . directed at away supporters throughout the game', and the unfurling of a banner in K Stand, under the scoreboard, complaining about United's manager, Alex Ferguson, which led to the police moving in and escorting someone out. Anti-management chants continued throughout the game. The officers then walked around the Piccadilly area but there was nothing further to note down.

Operation Mars was up and running. Over the next twelve months, these officers and others would follow United's hardcore element, seeking to make friends, overhear conversations, witness fights. The Palace game had been an uneventful start, but the next match, at home to Tottenham Hotspur on December 16, was more promising. The police observers saw an incident at half-time as six or seven Spurs fans queued at the pie stall under B Stand. A short, stocky man in a dark brown leather jacket threw the contents of a plastic beer glass over them. 'This appeared to be the signal to people around the Spurs fans and from all sides other males began to punch the Spurs fans,' recorded one of the undercover officers.

One of the United crew allegedly chased a Spurs fans up a stairway, shouting, 'Come on then you fucking coward, come back down and fight. Down here and see how hard you are.' When a uniformed police sergeant finally intervened, another United lad, in his mid-thirties and wearing a waxed Carlton jacket, shouted, 'It's the balding cunt we want. He's their main man.' One of the undercovers later wrote that a man 'believed to be Antony O'Niel' (sic) was also there. 'The other Spurs fans had not retaliated during the assault – the attack had been so quick and well co-ordinated that they had not had time,' recorded another officer. 'All the Spurs fans looked terrified,' wrote another.

Over the next few weeks, the officers went to Liverpool, Aston Villa and Wimbledon away. They recorded the odd sighting of a face they recognised or the occasional bit of snatched conversation in the crowd – like a young skinhead saying, 'We've got to get out early for the fight, we don't want to miss the fight' – at Anfield, but it amounted to little. It was clear that their knowledge of United's main faces was, at that stage, limited. At home games they tended to visit the same pubs – the Grey Parrot in Hulme, the Tollgate, Mother Macs, the Waggon and Horses – in the hope of latching on to some of the main boys.

A third round FA Cup tie against Nottingham Forest on 7 January 1990 was perhaps the turning point both for the football club and for Operation Mars. It later became famous as the match that saved Alex Ferguson's career: after a disastrous start to the season, the United manager faced the sack if they were knocked out of the cup (though chairman Martin Edwards would later deny it). Up stepped substitute striker Mark Robins, who came off the bench to score the only goal and put United through. They would go on to win the trophy and secure Ferguson's job.

The game also saw the Mars team start to assign names to identified, target figures: Alpha, Bravo, brothers Chaz and Delta, Echo, November. And, of course, Kilo.

The undercover spotters were out early at 8.15 at Piccadilly train station, clocking faces. Some got on the train with the lads, noting that a 'new' group of about eight United alighted at Sheffield. At Nottingham the group split into two. One mob of about fifty walked straight into the Queens pub, where they met a number of United supporters with southern accents. 'It appeared as though this was a pre-arranged meeting place,' recorded one of the officers.

Two of the lads were overheard talking. 'What a bad turnout for a cup match,' said one. 'Fifteen of us came and stopped last night and thirty more are coming. If it does go off, half of these in here won't fight.' Quite a few of the group repeatedly left the pub and then came back in; they were obviously watching for something.

PC John O., GMP Observation Log, Notts Forest v Man U, 7.1.90

The atmosphere inside the PH [public house] was very tense and at one stage (a) male in a sheepskin jacket came back into the PH and picked up an empty Pils bottle, holding it by the neck at his side. There were approximately 100–120 United supporters in the PH at this time.

My attention was drawn to three males stood near the bar. One of whom, a white male, late 20's, black hair and moustache, was said to be 'Scarrett' [notorious Forest hooligan Paul Scarrott].

A few of the United supporters left the PH and Bravo and Chaz went outside. They returned quickly and started to gather others around them. The next thing, two coloured males, mid 20's, one wearing a check jacket, entered the P.H. and remained at the doorway. The one in the check jacket began teasing the United supporters by saying, 'Ooh, what a lot.'

All the United fans turned to confront the two coloured males . . . at the forefront was target Chaz. The coloured male in the check jacket looked at Chaz and said, 'You were all mouth across the street. What are you going to do now?'

Chaz replied 'Fuck off you black bastard.' He then beckoned other members of the group with his hands and said 'Let's do them.'

The coloured male then said, 'You're only about fifteen, get to the fucking back.'

A United male in [a] ¾ length sheepskin coat . . . made his way to the front of the United group. He was holding a ½ pint tumbler glass (empty).

By this time Chaz picked up an empty pint glass. Chaz shouted at a [young] male with shoulder length scruffy hair wearing a flying jacket, 'Don't just sit there doing nothing. Fucking do him.'

At this point the male in the sheepskin threw the glass he was holding at the two coloureds, striking the one not wearing the check jacket on the side of the face. This action resulted in a number of bottles and glasses raining down on the coloured males, who hastily retreated out of the premises. The glass in the door was smashed by a bottle.

Almost immediately a uniformed police inspector and other police entered the premises and ordered everybody out. The United supporters spilled out into the street and started walking down the street immediately to the right. Up ahead were the two coloured males and two white males.

At the front of this group now walking along the road were Bravo, Chaz and Delta. We turned a corner and members of the group at the back turned around, causing the group to stop. Behind us were the same two coloured males and a white male. They were beckoning the United supporters to go back up the road. One of the United supporters said 'Don't go, it's a trap. If you go down there you'll get ambushed, there'll be hundreds of them.'

A number of police arrived and surrounded the United supporters, escorting them to the ground.

Spoke to a white male, 6' 0", Southern accent, thin build, brown hair, he said 'This happens every time. We should stick together instead of splitting up.'

The police escorted them to the ground but then left them. Some wandered back towards the city centre before meeting up again outside the Forest stand, where someone said, 'Meet here after the match, we're going to get Forest on the bridge as they come out.' United won the game 1–0 and outside the cops said any United fans wanting the trains should go to the left. 'Chaz and his group, with hundreds of others, went right towards Trent Bridge,' recorded the undercover officers. But the gang lost them in the side streets and vanished.

Another undercover, Paul D., who went to the game by car, got talking to some United fans in the Granby Hotel pub in Nottingham. They said that Tony O'Neill ran coaches from the Grey Parrot. When the cop asked if O'Neill was going to be there that day, one of them said, 'No, no, O'Neill's keeping his head down. The police are after him. They think he's the main man for everything so he's staying away.'

They also picked up that the Cockney Reds had split into two groups. 'A younger, more violent faction have emerged. They are only interested in violence and do not limit their fighting to rival fans.' This officer also caught up with the lads that the other cops had lost after the game and witnessed a confrontation between 100 Forest fans and sixty United:

> At station. Group of males on forecourt and Carrington Street. Large group of Notts Forest fans run from direct [sic] of bus station along Carrington Street. Begin to attack United fans in Carrington Street. Notts Forest contain high proportion of black males. Group of United fans run from station at Forest fans. Male at front of United fans is Stephen Ashton, target Alpha. Also part of group is Martin Gallagher, target Chaz. Boths sets of fans clash [and] fighting breaks out. People running into entry on opposite side to station to get away from fighting. Able to get close. Prevented by police. Fight broken up. United fans driven back onto station.

At a home game the following week, one of the undercovers talked briefly to Target Echo, who had thrown the bottle at the Forest fan in the pub. The officer, attempting to win his confidence, lapsed into racist jargon when he said, 'They were cheeky bastards, them coons at Nottingham last week, weren't they?'

Echo replied, 'Yes, they had a lot of bottle didn't they. They had some arse to do that but all they wanted was us to chase them onto the estate.' Asked about the glass incident he said, 'I asked if they were tooled up, they went [hand movement in pocket] so it had to be done.'

The next outbreak of trouble came at lowly Hereford United in the Cup on January 28. A mob of about 100 Hereford outside the Old Harp pub started shouting at United fans in a multi-storey car park. The United rained coins and cans down on them until the United charged, causing many of the Hereford to run off. Just as fighting was about to begin, another thirty or forty Hereford came from the direction of the Wellington pub. 'This caused the Man Utd fans to hesitate,' recorded one officer. 'One of the group said, 'Be careful, they're CID,' and pointed out two males who were stood on the junction, one of whom was wearing a deerstalker hat. 'This group then made their way towards the coach park.'

February 2 brought a much bigger fixture: Manchester City at Old Trafford. Given the recent history of violence between the two rivals, Operation Omega put five undercover officers out on the streets. Some watched the Cockney Reds arrive by train at Piccadilly. Another one went to the Merchants pub on Oldham Street before the game, while others observed a number of United boys meeting at the Imperial before moving on to Wetherby's.

At the ground one of them noted a small group stood near an exit, including Tony O'Neill. '[Target] Kilo is holding left hand palm downwards and making punching motions with right hand,' noted one officer. According to another, 'The atmosphere was very volatile with chanting and gestures being transferred between the two sets of supporters,' recorded one cop. In the second half, when City scored, numerous small fights broke out.

After the game, the undercovers watched Tony with a group of up to 180 United walking up Chester Road, stopping traffic. He then peeled off with three or four others and went straight up Chester Road, while the main group continued up Stretford Road. One officer then clocked him and the others walking up City Road towards the Grey Parrot in Hulme.

Officer Paul D. went to the Grey Parrot. 'Pub very full,' he wrote. 'In main lounge is Alpha, Kilo and Hotel. Stood between door and bar. Exit to bar. Shout from the doorway, "Come on, come on." Look round, Kilo is stood at door looking back towards pub. "It's time, fucking move, come on, move." All the people start to move towards the door. Alpha shouting, "Come in or we'll miss the blue shit." Most of the pub leave. Outside Kilo, Hotel and Alpha are marshalling everyone into one large group. Group sets off through the flats towards the Crescents.' The Crescents were several notorious, semi-circular blocks of flats in the Hulme area.

GMP Observation Log, Man Utd v Man City, 3.2.90

The group was approx 300–400 in strength. As the group moved it spread out, in a middle group I saw targets Bravo, Chaz and Delta and at the back target Echo. Leading the whole group were targets Kilo and Hotel.

From the Crescents into Otterbank Close, the group by this time was well spread out. I saw target Kilo face the group, raise his arms in the air and shout, 'Stop, stop.' Some of the group started chanting [but] Kilo shouted, 'Shut up or you'll give us away.' Hotel went to the side of the group and urged stragglers to hurry up, others shouted the same. Once the group bunched up, Kilo and Hotel led them off.

Lots of the group were carrying bottles, sticks and empty pint beer glasses. All the conversations were about attacking City fans and being seen by the police and what to do if they were split up. I heard somebody ask where they were going and I heard somebody reply, 'The Falcon.' The whole group walked over a footbridge and onto Epping Walk, Kilo and Hotel still leading the group.

At the end of Epping Walk, Kilo and Hotel turned to face the group, hands in the air, and stopped them, stragglers were told to hurry up. I heard Hotel say to people around him, 'Let's go for it, let's give it 'em as one.' The group then carried on, still led by Hotel and Kilo, alongside the Ardri Club.

Up to Cambridge Street where the group forced a bus to stop, until most had crossed the road. They then went alongside the Dental Hospital towards Oxford Road. Kilo and Hotel again stopped the group and waited till it bunched up. I then heard Kilo shout, 'We are going to go up here and turn right, keep together, keep quiet, we're nearly there.'

I then heard a male shout, 'Tony, Tony, here Tony, urgent.' I then saw a M/W, slim build, light coloured hair, 20's wearing a sweat shirt standing to my left, start to point towards myself and Paul and say, 'Hold on lads there's two sweets with us.' I did not know that a 'sweet' refers to a Police Officer. The crowd then opened up around us. I then heard Kilo shout, 'They're dibble, get them.'

I then tried to run back in the direction I had come from but I felt someone grab hold of the hood on the back of my coat. I then felt punches and kicks raining down on me, and I staggered into some railings, with kicks and blows still raining down on me. Most of the blows were to my head and face. I then heard someone say, 'That's enough, leave him.'

I then managed to stagger away from the group. As I did so I saw Paul pick himself up from the floor and start to go in the same direction I was going. I then joined Paul and we walked back to the Grey Parrot to pick up our vehicle.

To office and then to hospital to receive treatment. Received three stitches to my bottom lip.

THE MEN IN BLACK

The fighting continued that evening, with roving mobs of United and City seeking each other out in the city centre. Several pubs, including the Crown and Kettle and the Land o' Cakes, were trashed, and the carnage ended in near-fatality when a sixty-strong City mob attacked Wetherby's nightclub and beat a twenty-five-year-old United fan insensible. Gerald O'Connor was left lying in the gutter with serious head fractures and would spend six months in hospital learning to walk and talk again.

The next game, Millwall away, promised to be an equally challenging trip for the undercover spotters. They boarded the 9 a.m. train to London Euston with some of their targets, then snooped around a few pubs. Finding no-one of interest, they walked to Kings Cross and took the Tube to Whitechapel. On the train they heard a group of West Ham discussing a CCTV video of a fight between City and United on Chester Road that had been shown on TV. They also mentioned that a member of the ICF was organising a trip to Italy for the World Cup that summer,

At the ground one of the spotters sussed a group of 100 United fans around the visitors' turnstiles, again including some of his targets. At half-time some United moved across a segregation aisle to sit among Millwall supporters. Police moved them back. After the game United were held in for a short while before being escorted to New Cross Gate station. Tony O'Neill was on the train and was allegedly overheard saying, 'I've had a wicked day.' But the worst the spotters could report was some intelligence from a pub landlord that there had been some plans for United to 'wreck the Cyprus Tavern', a Manchester nightclub frequented by City thugs, as revenge for the previous game against their Blue rivals.

On February 18, two coaches left from the Grey Parrot at 9.15 a.m for the game against Newcastle. Some of the spotters had managed to get seats on one of the coaches, and saw O'Neill heading up in a silver estate car. Once in Newcastle, United mobbed up in a busy pub.

GMP Observation Log,
Newcastle Utd v Man Utd, 18.2.90

To Black Bull PH premises extremely crowded with a mixture of United and Newcastle fans.

On entering a small room to right of door saw approx 20 United fans inc November and July. Unknown male said, 'Gary, it's a good turnout.'

November replied, 'Yes, but where's Frothy and the other fuckers?'

After approx ten minutes November left complaining the pub was too crowded. Moved into main bar of PH. Saw target India wearing a black blazer stood with a half a dozen males, believed to be Cockneys.

Saw November on pavement opposite with a group of twenty United fans. I/c white male, mid 20's, 5' 10", long brown hair, plump build, target Oscar.

White, male previously seen working the door at the Grey Parrot. Target Papa and white male, mid-20's, med. Build, 5'8", brown hair parted in middle, which is permed and has blond streaks. Target Quebec. A few minutes later I was aware that groups were watching out of the window and then someone shouted, 'It's going off.' A crowd of people moved towards the door and a group of Newcastle fans hurried out of the pub.

I made way outside and opposite the pub on the junction of Wellington Street saw a white male unconscious in the road. Around him were Oscar, November, Papa and Quebec with other United fans.

A Newcastle fan shouted over, 'One Man U down.'

Although police were present the United and Newcastle fans were still goading each other. Crossed over and joined November's group. Oscar said to November, 'Gary, we did all right considering the numbers. There was more of them.'

Papa came over to November and pointed out a Newcastle fan saying 'Gary, that's the fucker who did him.'

November replied, 'I don't care what he's done, we don't get anyone nicked. We'll sort it.'

I then struck up a conversation with an unknown member of the group. On asking what had happened he replied, 'It went off and Ernie got fucking twatted. Look at him, he's spark out.'

By now a group of approx fifty United fans had congregated on the corner, groups of Newcastle fans were moving through them.

A young Newcastle fan came over and said, 'Get your mob together and get up here, come on,' obviously an invitation to fight. Police moved in with dogs. The United fans then moved en masse across the road towards a park where a group of Newcastle fans were gathering. Unknown members of the group were making remarks such as 'Come on Reds, let's fucking do it.' The situation was becoming extremely volatile.

Large numbers of police moved in between the two groups and forced the United fans back down towards the ground.

As they moved reluctantly back down the road, Newcastle fans were on the banking to our left goading the United fans to fight. On nearing the ground a Newcastle fan was stood on the pavement threatening the passing United fans. The United fans immediately in front of us kicked him as they walked past. He made no effort to retaliate.

The Newcastle fans followed along the embankment to our left and there were groups in the road to our right. Even though the group were under police escort several of the group tried to get up the embankment but were pushed back by police. One Newcastle fan up the banking shouted 'Come on, what's the fucking matter with you, you shit.'

The United fans were moved on by the police, as they did the Newcastle fan threw a bottle which narrowly missed us and struck a male walking ahead of us. Police then chased the male and detained him. A group of United fans then rushed into the roadway and started fighting with Newcastle fans. Several punches and kicks were thrown before the police separated them. Included in this group were Oscar and Quebec.

On reaching the ground the United fans gathered in a large group and more fighting looked imminent until the police forced United fans off the road and up towards the ground.

On the car park saw India and March together. Entered ground and seating area reserved for United fans. Below us in seats saw targets November, Quebec, Hotel, Oscar.

During first half during which the crowd were extremely agitated a scuffle broke out and Quebec was spoken to by police.

At half-time down under stand saw targets Bravo, India, July, Kilo, November, Oscar, Quebec. Spoke to two unknown males about fighting prior to game.

Back into stand during second half crowd continued in a volatile manner. Several times Newcastle fans ran onto the pitch and several arrests or ejections were made.

After game, left ground. No incidents

THE MEN IN BLACK

GMP Observation Log, Chelsea v Man Utd, 24.2.90

Into Trafalgar pub [on the Kings Road, west London], full of United supporters many of them Cockneys. In all I would estimate approx 150 United fans present. Inside pub saw target Kilo talking to two Cockney males who by their hand movements appeared to be giving him directions.

One was male, 40 yrs, Mediterranean appearance (see Hereford log). The second male 30–35 yrs olive complexion, 6'2", prop build, black hair greying slightly. Smart casual dress. Also in pub were the targets India, July, Romeo, Tango, Summerfield, male with M.U.F.C scroll on neck, group from Yorkshire.

Kilo then moved to the opposite side of the pub and sat with a white male, late teens, shoulder length hair, glasses. He was also joined by Summerfield, Bravo and Delta. Whilst we were stood near the door a white male, late teens, blond curly hair, Yorkshire accent came into the pub and started talking to a group next to us. John O said to him, 'What's happening?' The youth now target 'Uniform' replied, 'They know we are here, I've been up to the Man In The Moon. There are two hundred of them.' He then moved from group to group inside the pub.

There was constantly a group of twenty to thirty males outside on the pavement and guarding the door. It became apparent the group were expecting to be attacked. We moved from the door further inside the pub. Uniform then joined two other Yorkshire males.

1) White male, 25 years, dark hair, moustache, XTG shirt, target Vole.
2) White male, 18 years, blond hair, target Whiskey.

I then visited the gents, there was two unknown males inside. One turned to the other laughing and said, 'I needed to have a piss before it goes off.' Returned to bar.

The group stood outside all came into the pub, into the bar area. At this someone from the main room shouted 'Let's go.' At which the whole of the gang left the pub, several of them picking up glasses and bottles as they left.

Leaving the pub the group approx 150 strong turned right walking down Kings Road. A number of police arrived in vans and began to monitor the group. Almost immediately approx 20 crossed the road and walked on the opposite side.

We were near the back of the group, directly in front of us was targets Kilo, Bravo and Chaz. On reaching Beaufort Street, Kilo and approx 10 others crossed over to the opposite side of the road. This group increased their pace and got ahead. A short time later the main group crossed over and fell in behind the leading group led by Kilo, Bravo, Chaz, Delta, March, Uniform, Vole and Whisky.

We had walked a short distance when a shout went up from the front and the whole gang started running diagonally across the road towards the Man In The Moon pub. Several police No Waiting signs and bottles were thrown by the people at the front of the gang at the pub windows. One of the front windows cracked. After a brief hesitation in the middle of the road, the front of the gang continued across to the pub. One youth again picked up a yellow police cone and started hitting the cracked window with it in an attempt to smash the cracked window. I could see several people inside the pub and the street was crowded with ordinary shoppers. Almost immediately as it had begun the mayhem ceased as more police arrived.

The group continued down Kings Road chanting

'Manchester,' members of the gang were shouting 'Stick together, keep it tight' and shouting for the people at the front to slow down. At one stage those at the back of the group stopped to confront some Chelsea fans behind us. One Cockney male shouted, 'Come on, let's do them again,' but the front of the gang continued on so they turned and followed. Saw target Tango being stopped by the police.

To ground outside saw targets Kilo, Bravo, India, Chaz in a large group outside the away supporters' entrance. Many of these didn't have tickets. The group was in an agitated state.

One Cockney Red shouted, 'If we kick it off they've got to let us in.'

Stood next to Cockney male, Mediterranean appearance. A young Cockney Red came over to him and said, 'Come on, there's only a few of them, if we all walk off down a side street they'll follow us then we can turn and do them.' He then started pointing out Chelsea supporters who he said he knew.

Enter ground approx 70 fans locked out.

Another officer also described the attack on the pub in his log: 'When the main group reached Beaufort Street, Kilo crossed over the road followed by about ten others. He speeded up and got in front of the main group. A short time later the main group joined Kilo and his group. Kilo was then at the front of the group. This group included Bravo, Chaz, Delta, India, July, March, Uniform and Vole. Also Cockney Reds.

'A shout went up from the front and the whole gang ran across the road towards the Man in the Moon pub. I saw traffic cones hitting the windows, I heard glass smashing, I could see March in the thick of it by the main door of the pub, then my view was blocked. The group carried on along the road, I saw

Chaz leap up and kick a shop window. The whole window shook but did not break. The Kings Road was very busy with afternoon shoppers and a lot of people would have been terrified of this group rampaging through the street. Lots of extra police arrived and tried to sort the group out.'

The Operation Mars officers felt they were making headway. Before a home game against Luton Town, they allegedly overheard Tony O'Neill in the Dog and Partridge pub as he enquired about a United fan badly injured during the fighting against Man City at the previous derby game. 'How's the poor lad on the life support machine?' asked O'Neill. He then mentioned the trip to London for the Chelsea match: 'We wasted them at Euston, there was Chelsea and Tottenham. We had trouble at the Underground. There was cops everywhere but we still had a go. Getting to the Trafalgar, they all left together after the shout went up. We walked past their pub. The police were with us but we still hit it, then they took us to the ground.'

Large numbers of Reds without tickets made the short journey to Sheffield United on 10 March 1990. Sheffield's Blades Business crew was one of the more active hooligan mobs in the league at that time, and trouble was anticipated. Just before kick-off it became apparent that United fans had infiltrated the Spion Kop terrace reserved for home supporters. About seventy were chanting in the bottom corner of the terrace. Just after kick-off, fighting broke out on the Kop around the United contingent and some of the United fans started to climb over the perimeter fence onto the pitch side. Police escorted them back to Bramhall Lane and placed them in an empty terrace below the West Wing Stand; the group were applauded by their fellow Mancunians as they were marched around the pitch. About five minutes later, another group of United fans were taken from the John Street terrace.

At the end of the game, which United won 1–0, Reds fans

taunted their Sheffield rivals as they left the John Street terrace and threw punches over the fence separating them before police moved in to keep them apart. A gang of 100–150 United, with many of the Operation Mars targets at the front, were then followed by spotters as they walked to the railway station. Once there, a breakaway group of fifty walked to the bus station looking for a fight. They were later seen being chased away by mounted officers. A group of Sheffield then turned up at the train station shouting, 'Come on Man U,' but police with dogs prevented fighting.

On March 18, Liverpool played at Old Trafford. During the game, individual Liverpool fans in B Stand were threatened, and afterwards the police saw around 200 United gather at the junction of Warwick Road and Chester Road, outside the chip shops. The Liverpool supporters were then escorted along Warwick Road, and as they appeared the group began to chant 'United!' and surged towards the escort. The police moved them off but they reassembled in the centre of the road by the central barrier.

About ten Liverpool fans broke away from the escort and walked up Chester Road towards Stretford. 'This immediately captured the attention of the United group who began to move towards them, climbing over the central barrier,' recorded one of the spotters. They shadowed them to a blue minibus parked outside Charlie Browns Exhaust Centre. 'When they reached it there was a standoff situation until a roar went up and the United supporters charged at them,' wrote the spotter John O. 'Target Uniform was next to me and was shouting, "Go on, get the bastards." As he moved towards the central reservation, he was limping slightly because he had just fell [sic] over dropping his chips and beans when climbing over the central barrier.'

Twenty or thirty United attacked the Liverpool group. 'I saw one Liverpool fan wearing a white shirt being kicked and punched,' recorded another undercover, Derek M. 'He had his back to the garage wall and was attempting to fight back but was overwhelmed by numbers. Police arrived almost immediately . . .'

The officers found little to report at the next few games, other than a mildly comic incident when United played Oldham Athletic in a Sunday cup game at Maine Road. The undercovers spotted Tony O'Neill and described him as 'drunk or drugged, in very high spirits.' One of them, Simon C., claimed O'Neill put his arm around him and said, 'Hiya mate, how are you?'

'What about the Liverpool result?' asked Simon C., trying to make conversation.

'Fucking Scouse bastards, let's kill any Scousers that get in our way,' was the response.

There was little more by way of violence over the next two months, up to and including the FA Cup final against Crystal Palace on May 12. Target Kilo was seen being marched out of the standing area at Tottenham in April by three uniformed Met officers, but the Manchester undercover team did not record why. The season culminated in United winning the FA Cup, but finishing a highly disappointing thirteenth in the league.

Chapter Three

BUSTED

THE 1990–91 SEASON began, as always, with the Charity Shield at Wembley. Manchester United were playing League Champions Liverpool, a fixture that in the past would have been X-rated for potential disorder. But since Heysel in 1985 and the appalling Hillsborough Disaster in 1989, the prospect of Liverpool fans causing trouble had massively diminished. Nevertheless, the Operation Mars officers were out on the streets, in particular keeping tabs on the large number of United fans drinking around the Irish pubs of Kilburn. Tony O'Neill was seen 'in a very good mood . . . visiting a number of groups whilst at the [pub].' But, as expected, there was little trouble at the game.

The first few home games of the league season were just as uneventful. The undercover officers seemed to spend their time traipsing around pubs before the game where nothing was happening and then trying to tag along behind any of the lads they recognised at the game. It was clear they'd made very little headway in penetrating the inner reaches of the United mob. While they could now identify key faces, and could occasionally get near enough to them to overhear snatches of conversation or even exchange the odd few words, they were nowhere near being taken into their confidence.

A trip to Leeds United for the first away game, however, promised the breakthrough they needed. Leeds, whose fans detested their Manchester enemies with a passion, had just returned to the top division and the game at Elland Road would give them the opportunity to resume their extraordinary hatred of Manchester United. The game, on August 28, was an evening kick-off, and United assembled a formidable mob of their biggest hitters at a service station on the M62 motorway before heading into Leeds to do battle. Yet somehow the undercover officers would miss two of the biggest fights for years.

GMP Observation Log, Leeds v Man Utd, 28.8.90

Leave (Victoria) station, travel to Hartshead Moor Services, M62, Eastbound. On the car park were approximately 150–200 Manchester United supporters. I observed targets Bravo, Lima, Kilo, November, Oscar, Quebec. Within minutes of our arrival, the group began to board their cars and approximately 20–25 cars set off in convoy off the services area.

Travel to Leeds where on the A58 Halifax to Leeds Road I observed a gang of 150–200 males walking towards LUFC. Right at the front were targets Kilo and Oscar. The gang were then led left into Gelderd Road before turning right under the motorway subway to LUFC.

I was in a position to observe the gang walk past the visitors' turnstiles and then along the back of the South Stand. At this point, target Kilo detached himself from the main gang who had now stopped behind the South Stand. Kilo crossed the road and began to walk in between the cars that were parked on the car park. He stopped temporarily and began looking all around before rejoining the main group.

The group then marched past the Old Peacock public house where a great number of Leeds supporters were congregated. They passed a row of shops where I could see members of the Manchester United gang beckoning the Leeds supporters with their hands.

The group then walked through the gates that lead into the area behind the West Stand. This area was congested with Leeds supporters.

After a few minutes, the gang returned out of this area. Again, targets Kilo and Oscar were leading, closely followed by November and Bravo. The gang went back towards the visitors' turnstiles.

The Leeds fans were incensed by this action by the United gang. They were complaining that they (M.U.) shouldn't be allowed to get away with walking onto their end. (L.U.) also said that if they (L.U.) had done the same at Old Trafford they would be happy.

The Manchester gang then congregated across the road from the visitors' turnstiles . . . Enter South Stand where I noticed target Kilo in the refreshment area. He was looking out of the windows which overlook the main road . . .

Leave the ground minutes before full time. Outside at the back of the car park, a gang of Leeds supporters had congregated, numbering approximately 60–80. They were moved on by the police. I overheard one Leeds fan talking to another, he said 'It's no use going into town, they didn't come by train.'

Eventually we made our way to Gelderd Road and passed the Wheatsheaf public house, where a number of Leeds supporters had congregated outside.

We returned to this area a short while later to find that this group had dispersed and that there were a number of police vehicles present.

Drive along the A58 Halifax Road where at a layby near to some houses there appeared to be some kind of disturbance between the residents and young males. No one identified.

Visit Hartshead Services. Target Oscar amongst group of approximately 20 leaving services.

TONY: Okay, if we're going to Leeds then we'll have to change our tactics for this night game, as I'm sick of the sheepshaggers always claiming to want to kick our heads in but they always seem to abuse small groups and the odd fan. So it's down to us to take it to them. We have to have a meeting point arranged and also a drop-off point, so off set one of the lads a few weeks before. He drives from Manchester and checks various routes for us to drive to the place where we have called it on with Leeds. Our destination is the Wheatsheaf pub, which is well away from the ground and easily accessible. Getting there undetected is the problem. Also we are putting our lives at risk, as this encounter, if it goes wrong, could be the end of most of us. Leeds and Manchester viciously hate each other, so there are going to be no prisoners.

To do this right we have to outwit the police. Now, outwitting the Yorkshire Old Bill is not a problem – I don't think you have to outwit them, but you, the reader, can decide on that one. Our problem is the Manchester police. How do we avoid getting sussed before we get to Yorkshire? We discuss the options, a couple of routes, and it is decided that everyone has to go in cars and meet at Hartshead Moor service station on the M62, then come off at the next junction, the A58, and turn right and stay on the road till the end. And when is the end? Well, that's my job, as I'm in the lead car which leaves Hartshead Moor with my little pal, and Mario driving.

On Hartshead Moor service station are over 180 lads all ready for this move. This is what it's all about. Knowing we were going for this meet with Leeds, not knowing how many of them would be waiting and what kind of weapons were going to be used, my whole body was building up to a nervous breakdown. My legs were weak, my stomach was turning over and I was feeling sick. There was not much talking on that service station, as most who were there were feeling the same as me, except for one person, and that was Wing, who for twenty-five years has never shut up. Wing could and would talk to a cat if it stood still long enough. Football violence is his game and talking about it is his passion, a fucking nightmare to your brain after a minute. We were 180 lads now on a journey to the ultimate fight, something we had been doing for years, not hiding behind the police or making excuses. This was it. The total allocation for United's fans that night was just 800, so we had done brilliantly even to get tickets.

The route we took was uneventful apart from the occasional red light, which everyone simply drove straight through; there was no stopping, as being split up would have meant disaster. We pulled up about a mile from the Wheatsheaf on the edge of some estate near some industrial units and I got out first. Then it hit me. The excitement and all the day's tension got hold of me and I suddenly collapsed on the grass verge, unable to get up under the stress. It doesn't matter how many fights you have been in, when you're in those situations the tension can do very strange things, and on this occasion I lost the use of my legs for several seconds. It was actually half-comical, and the little fellow and Mario and myself burst out laughing. It soon passed as the buzz changed. There they all were, pulling up and jumping out of cars, bouncing up and down, eager to get on their way. Half an hour before kick-off, dark, no police, just a top firm on the march going to the pub for one almighty row.

Leeds had been told on a few occasions that we were coming and not to worry, we would get there no matter what, so just wait. Well the tension must have got to them too because as we came round the corner in the dark, about 500 yards away you could see them streaming across the road, heading towards the ground. Why they didn't wait I don't know, maybe they thought it was a blag and we were already at the ground, but we have always fronted it up – that's why all the others hate us. If there was no United then there would have been no fun.

We stopped on the pavement for a few seconds to get everyone tight so we could work out what was happening, then realised they hadn't spotted us, so off we went. We were now virtually running to get to them. It didn't take long for some of their stragglers to see us coming but there was nothing they could do, we were now round the corner and behind them. Leeds tried to run around and have a go but in the dark and not organised they had no chance of stopping us. We were into their backs and smacking them. Whoever tried to stand got it or was trampled. All they could do was carry on running as we chased them down under a bridge, where a few coppers tried to intervene. This kept on for another 200 yards until we had to turn right near the ground, where the police, who were now swinging the truncheons about, stopped us. No one argued about it, stop we did. No need to piss off the coppers. We had done what we had set out to do, plus no nickings, so why piss them off?

Leeds carried on, which led them under the subway at the ground, the very way we were going to go. We knew it would be hostile once we were through there but no-one was going to fuck us now. The police tried to cordon off the route but as we came through it was the same old story with Leeds: half-bricks and stones came flying at us and a few were struck, but at Elland

Road you expect that. The place was going mad: noise, pushing and shoving, and every now and then some daft Yorkshire cunt who tried to mingle in was bowled over and trampled.

Getting in the ground was no problem as the police surrounded the small area by the entrance. Once in, the relief was evident as everyone was laughing and joking about it all, people were asking who had done what, it was a carnival atmosphere. Those who'd missed it wanted to know what had happened. It was great: the plan had worked.

I don't remember the game or score, it didn't matter, the only thing now was getting home, and getting home together was the main event. We knew we were going to get kept in for twenty minutes or so, which meant Leeds would be waiting along the route to get revenge – which was only right.

The game ended and there were thousands outside United's end going mental, wanting to kill us, which was normal for Leeds as they are stuck in the Seventies. We were kept back for longer than twenty minutes but eventually everything was cleared. We had all got together at the gates and came out and turned left to head towards the subway. The coaches were on the other side, so we walked with those who were going to board them back to Manchester. The police were heavy in their presence and kept their eye on us, and we thought they'd stay with us all the way and try to intercept the inevitable attack along the route from Leeds. But you wouldn't believe it: as we went past the coaches they stopped to make sure those boarding were safe, but watched as our firm, hell-bent on trouble, walked off up the road. That's how thick these Yorkies were and that's the problem with the police: obey orders, don't think for yourself.

I am not going to lie. Even though this was a good firm of lads, I and many others were worried. Things could go badly wrong, so with a few instructions to each other and a lot of nervous banter, we all got tight together and headed to the top of the road and turned left, back onto the road where we had earlier given Leeds a hiding.

We marched on the pavement and could see the Wheatsheaf pub again in the far distance. The road was clear but we hadn't gone under the bridge yet and we were still mainly in the dark. As we passed each little street to our right, we thought it would come, but it didn't. Not until we were past the bridge did we see them emerging from in and around the Wheatsheaf. They charged down the road, and it was a frightening sight, but also a thrill.

We quickly got in the road and all kept close, just walking towards this charge. There was no ducking out of this one. Leeds were now all over the road but were not together like us. The first fifteen or twenty were well ahead of the others and were coming straight at us. We suddenly charged at them and they were down. I went past their front line with several others and everyone followed. We started exchanging punches and kicks but we were moving forward and always giving it to them. They were now scattering. One lad was getting his head badly smashed on a barrier, but no sympathy there; you went down on this occasion and you knew what to expect, so no bleating from us. There were some boots going in, especially to that first lot.

We were now all over the road, the pub, the car park, chasing them until the police arrived. The fact that we were outnumbered had worked in our favour, making us concentrate more. They had too many and had no organisation from their lads, who we lost respect for that night, not because they ran, we've all done that, but because as we all got to our cars and headed off towards Hartshead Moor service station for a debriefing – not my words on the night but Wing's (you've got to laugh) – some of Leeds's so-called top boys were trying to snipe one of the cars with four of the lads in. They got a little shock and were well and truly fucked off with the help of some car tools. But when the police intervened, the Leeds grassed us up. Not only that, they went to the police station and made statements.

The rendezvous back at Hartshead Moor thirty minutes later was unbelievable. Anyone who has ever been involved in something like that will understand what was going on, all the backslapping and laughter. Even those who had been bloodied were loving it, maybe the most. We'd done Leeds good and proper.

The police that night had seen us on the service station earlier and had taken photos of us as part of their undercover work, but hadn't been able to stop the night's activities. Or was that their intention? The undercover work was a strange one, as they knew we knew who they were and if we couldn't see them then probably they were thereabouts.

It worked that time, but the next time we went to Leeds we tried the same plan again and it all went wrong. We used the same route, via Hartshead Moor, and there was about the same number of us. But this time we got there too early and when we walked past the Wheatsheaf it was quiet. We didn't think anyone was there but suddenly they came charging down the road behind us. They piled straight into United, with a few police trying to stop it, and had us running all the way down the road until we got round the corner, where we got back together and held it.

Leeds had a good day that day. The truth is they have had a few good days against us, just as we have had a few against them. They did have a lot more than us and had all the bricks and everything, and there were people getting hit on the head with bottles. Once we had started to back off it was not easy to stop the rot against that kind of attack.

But all the time we were going there in those days we were getting only 800–1,200 tickets. And that is when the straight members wouldn't go because Leeds was such a scary place for them. We kept going year after year and eventually sorted it out.

Now the straight members get all the tickets and we can't get any.

———————

For the next nine games, the undercover officers continued to observe their targets but once again saw little, if any, disorder. Indeed, the visit of lowly Wrexham for a night game on October 23 was their first little bit of excitement for weeks, when about fifty of the visitors had a scuffle in the doorway of the Toll Gate pub when they were refused entry. Manchester City on October 27 was expected to be of a different order – and would lead, unexpectedly, to the arrest of their number one target.

TONY: Being part of a firm of lads and being one of its main faces has its drawbacks, one of them being having to contend with the police week after week since football intelligence started out on us around 1988. Their job is to gather evidence on your activities to get a conviction and hopefully imprisonment. This leads to the majority of coppers getting to know you, but not you knowing them. It also leads them to hate you and think it is their duty to arrest you for fuck all, as in my case on many occasions.

We had played Man City and that evening I and several hundred United fans settle in a pub called The Ship on the edge of Salford and the city centre. We all know that we're going nowhere because of the police presence outside so we settle down to having a laugh and to enjoy the beer. After a couple of hours we are in full flow. A few locals are stuck in the corner of another room but we're not bothering them and they're happy.

Well, in any large gathering in these situations something happens, and this was no exception. Three lads start arguing but it is quickly resolved with me and one of the others intervening. Unbeknown to us, one of the local women has gone outside and started gobbing off to the plod, who have been sat there bored shitless for several hours. They now join the throng in the pub. As they walk in everything goes quiet. They walk around but we were happy where we were and no-one is mouthing off, which leaves the police with no excuse to throw us out. They are in a dilemma until they round the corner and there I am, stood ignoring them. Bingo.

This twat of a copper has suddenly got me in a head-lock and he is dragging me head first towards the vault door, pursued by all the other coppers. They haul me outside and the next thing I am over the bonnet of a cop car. Reinforcements arrive and they start going ballistic on everyone. I endure what the police call justifiable force, which in plain language is a few punches to the stomach, a few boots to the legs, head smashed on the car and a form of torture in which my arms are raised behind my back and vertically stretched from the sockets. It has always baffled me that when they are trying to rip your arms off they carry on screaming at you to stop resisting arrest so they can put the cuffs on you. Yet you're not resisting arrest, and the reason they can't cuff you is that they have got your arms above your head while you're doubled over. All this time, you're in agony trying not to scream or in some cases start crying.

I am slung into the back of a van, carted off, locked up and bailed on Monday with the same old story to my missus, 'I've not done anything,' so there's another four days without a meal cooked and clothes washed. But I knew in my head that the Football Intelligence would have been around with their cameras – and that could work in my favour.

For several more games the Operation Mars team found little to report. But their bosses and the Crown Prosecution Service must have been happy that they had already gathered enough evidence to make a mass prosecution stick. On 22 November 1990, the *Manchester Evening News* broke the news:

> More than 30 suspected Manchester United hooligans were arrested in a series of dawn swoops today.
>
> It was the culmination of a 15-month undercover operation by the Omega squad, which was set up by Manchester police to combat soccer violence.
>
> Homes in Manchester, London, Leeds, Barnsley, Bedford and Middlesex were raided.
>
> The suspects, who were believed to include a teacher and a man with close connections to Manchester police, were being questioned at nine police stations this afternoon.
>
> Officers recovered knives, baseball bats and other weapons.
>
> Some of those arrested are understood to belong to two gangs – the Cockney Reds and the Young Munichs, a sick reference to the air disaster of 1958.
>
> Further arrests are expected soon.
>
> Assistant Chief Constable Malcolm George . . . said that it was thought the operation had uncovered the 'generals' who led and guided the hooligans in skirmishes across the country.
>
> 'We believe we have identified the ringleaders and taken them out of the situation,' said Mr George.
>
> Violent incidents in Liverpool, Norwich, Hereford, Newcastle and Manchester were being investigated.

The dawn raids had finally come. Tony O'Neill and the rest were hauled from their beds in the early hours and taken in for questioning under caution. Tony was interviewed on the day he was arrested by a detective, with a PC in attendance, at Longsight Police Station in Manchester. Twenty-four names of his alleged co-conspirators were put to him, one by one. He denied knowing any of them. 'I might know them by face but not by name,' he said. He was then asked about the Manchester City game on 23 September 1989, which had directly led to Operation Mars.

Q At 2 p.m. that day you were seen at the Grey Parrot public house by police officers. There were approximately five hundred people there at the time. It is alleged . . . you led those five hundred people away from that pub up Upper Lloyd Street towards Manchester City's football ground. Is that correct?

A What do you mean led?

Q You were at the front of the crowd. Is that correct?

A I never led nobody. I may have been at the front of a group – which I can't recall – but that doesn't mean I led anybody.

Q Was it your intention to lead these people to attack the Clarence public house?

A My intention was to go on that day or any other day to watch a football match.

Q During the match there was a disturbance in the North Stand. A large number of United supporters had entered the stand reserved for City supporters and fighting broke out. Were you amongst that?

A No, I was not there. Nothing to do with me.

He was asked about several other games but denied ever being involved in trouble. 'I've never caused a disturbance at Old Trafford in twenty years of watching Manchester United,' he said. He was then quizzed about the Manchester City game on 3 February 1990:

Q   Prior to that match did you go to the Grey Parrot public house?

A   Yes.

Q   You were seen to arrive at 11 a.m. Why would you go there so early in the morning?

A   I can't remember being there.

Q   At 1.50 p.m. that day, two large groups were seen to leave the Grey Parrot. It is alleged by police officers that you were leading one of those groups from the public house. Was that correct?

A   I might have been at the front of any group but it doesn't mean to say I'm leading a group.

Q   You were seen to leave (Piccadilly) railway station with 150–200 persons. Again, you were at the front. What were you doing there?

A   Can't remember being there.

Q   Did you go down Oldham Street?

A   I've been down Oldham Street many a time for a drink.

Q   Did you go into the Merchants public house that day?

A   I might have done for a drink. Then again, I can't remember.

Q   What happened in the pub that day?

A   Can't remember.

Q   Was there a fight in there?

A   Was I fighting?

Q   Yes.

A   No.

Q   Did you take those supporters to that public house?

A   I did not take anybody anywhere.

Q   It's alleged that whilst you were at the Grey Parrot you went into the lounge and shouted to all the other supporters, 'It's time, fucking move, come on, move.' Is that correct?

A   No.

Q   During the match, were you bragging about your exploits at what happened at that public house a short time before?

A   Where was I bragging?

Q   Inside the ground.

A   Whereabouts?

Q   Under the stand.

A   No.

Q   So you wouldn't be making any actions showing your exploits?

A   Actions?

Q   Punching signs.

A   I might have been making actions about a boxing match – anything. Punching doesn't mean to say fighting. I might have been describing anything 'cos I weren't fighting that day. I never punched anyone that day.

Q   It is alleged that you went back to the Grey Parrot public house and on the way back you were overheard to say, 'If it goes like we planned it will be a good night.' Did you say anything like that?

A   Overheard by whom?

Q   By a police officer.

A   I never said anything like that.

Q   At 6.30 p.m. that night, it is alleged that you left the Grey Parrot public house with numerous other Manchester United fans and that again you were the leader of this group. It is alleged that you said to them, 'Come on, come on,' urging the other fans to come with you. Is that correct?

A   That's not correct.

Q   There were about 300 persons in that public house. Nearly all of them left with you. Most of them were carrying empty bottles and glasses from the pub. Why should they do that?

A   People, sometimes when they leave a public house, still have a drink on them. Why they left I don't know. When they left I can't remember. Being in the public house I can't remember.

Q It is alleged by police officers that you led this group from the public house into the Crescent area of Hulme. Is that correct?

A Me being at the front does not mean I led anyone. Being at the front just means I happened to be there.

He was asked about the attack on the two undercover officers, the fighting on the Kings Road before the Chelsea match, the rendezvous at Hartshead Moor services before Leeds, but the questioning was fruitless. He was also shown video surveillance footage and was asked to identify faces in it, but again declined. Nonetheless, the Crown Prosecution Service believed they had enough evidence to make the charges stick. Twenty-four men were accused of conspiring to riot at football matches, and were barred from attending any football matches in the UK.

Especially damning for Tony were the allegations that he ordered the attack on the two undercover officers – something he strongly denied – and the rampage down the Kings Road at Chelsea, which they claimed he had led. Yet after the initial flurry of activity, the wheels of justice stalled. It would be another eighteen months before the case would reach court. In the meantime, Tony faced charges over the incident at The Ship.

TONY: The police are only human, so they carry all the characteristics of us mere mortals: jealousy, envy, deceit, stupidity – and stupidity is the one in this case. I was charged with violent disorder over the incident in The Ship. They claimed I was involved in a large-scale disturbance inside the pub in which glasses and furniture were thrown at the police. I am told I'm looking at five years. Things look bad, but in the end I'm the only one happy.

It wasn't football intelligence officers that arrested me, it was the ordinary heavy mob. But I know that wherever I usually go on a football day, the football intelligence are somewhere watching. So I take the chance of instructing my solicitors to apply for any video footage of the incident outside The Ship public house. This request was made to the football intelligence unit, not to the cops who had arrested me. Unbelievably they declare they do have footage, and some time down the line they send it to us. It clearly shows the bird coming out of the pub complaining to the vanload of coppers, who then are seen walking into the pub and then me exiting by another door, getting thrown on the car bonnet, then all the commotion of the police forcing everyone out. This video is significant because it contradicts one of the coppers' statements, which then puts the rest of them in doubt.

But first up we have a PC giving evidence and this copper hasn't got a clue what's coming his way. He denies knowing me or where I live, even when we ask him if he knows Wythenshawe and specifically Gladeside Road, where my house was. 'No,' he replies. He also denies knowing Elaine and John, who live three doors away from me.

He continues in this vein for a few minutes, when suddenly he reacts as though I've just jumped out of the dock and twatted him with a hammer. He realizes the game is up, and the reason is because he regularly came to my street and visited my neighbours because he and friends used to meet there before going out hunting with dogs; not only that, he came into contact with my family in the house and on many occasions saw me. So there he is, stood rigid, looking at the ceiling and now admitting all the things he has just denied.

At this point I was rolling about with joy, not only at his discomfort but also at the jury, as this made them all lean forward and pay attention. You could see them all through the trial loving it; nothing complicated, just a good story of violence, injuries and chaos and as each day came and went you could see they were unravelling the deceit from the police.

The only problem I could see for me was the judge, because at this point he should have stopped the trial, but he carried on. This turned out to be even better for me, as the next copper in the witness box also said he did not know who I was. Now, I've done my homework and gone through all my court cases and any statements from them and also the statements for my court case to come for Operation Mars. I find a four-page statement from Operation Mars with his name on it. In it, he clearly states on several occasions he has seen me leading 250 United fans fighting and causing disorder in Manchester. Out of the 250 people he can only name me. So here he is denying knowing me in court, but we have proof from this statement he wrote eighteen months before. He does not yet know this, and several times denies knowing me. My barrister is in full flow and I believe is loving it more than me, as he is ready to pass the copper the incriminating documents to read.

As he reads them you actually see the blood drain from his face. Bang! The bells are ringing in his head, he's fucked and he knows it. The documents are passed to the judge and he now knows, but not the jury; they're left scratching their heads because the next thing the police idiot standing there starts to admit knowing me. Now the jury are totally fucked, they don't know what's going on.

Here's where the jealousy and stupidity come together in the police force. The foot soldier's lot is not always a happy one but if you're running around with the Intelligence Department it's cushy, so to keep it that way one lot doesn't tell the other lot what they're doing, so they can pretend they're superior. This leads to the jealousy, so no information is passed between them.

The video I had applied for from the intelligence unit from

outside the pub that night arrives in time for court. So one police department has given me this video without telling the prosecution or the arresting officers. Problem is, the prosecution ask to see it before we go in. We let them and the coppers look at it, and after viewing it they all come out smiling and laughing, saying, 'Yeah, there's fuck all on there. No problem.'

Well, there was something on the video. One of the officers testified it was the worst pub fight he had ever been involved in, with pint pots, bottles and glasses bouncing off his helmet, and in fact it was only his helmet that saved him from serious injury. Yet on the video you could clearly see him walking behind the Inspector into the pub – with no helmet on. So it couldn't be true. When I'd applied for the video, the FI hadn't told their fellow officers that I had this evidence, so they were totally wrong-footed. The five days in court went from bad to worse for the cops, and once again I was acquitted.

They finally charged twenty-eight of us on Operation Mars, so for the next few months my home became the centre for the defence. I got all the statements, all the photographs and all the videos and would regularly have ten people in my front room reviewing them. We compared the statements to the videos to the photographs, and made a note of any anomalies.

We were on curfews from early evening to the next morning every day, had to sign on at a police station three times a week, and couldn't attend any football matches. At the same time, United were blazing through Europe on the way to winning the European Cup Winners' Cup against Barcelona at the Feyenoord Stadium in Rotterdam, with Sparky Hughes scoring the goals. I couldn't miss the final, so I booked a week's holiday over there and got to the game. Surprisingly there was no comeback. The police in those days could come round to your house to check if you were in but they didn't and I got away with it. I was the only one on a curfew and ban who went.

Eventually the curfews were dropped because it was all dragging on so long.

People have asked me how much effect Mars had on United's firm. The answer is, not that much. For example, in 1992, while the case was still on-going, we played Nottingham Forest in the League Cup final at Wembley. Forest's firm obviously saw this as their big chance to do United, and put together what was apparently one of their biggest ever mobs. Back then, a lot of United would drink in Kilburn on a cup final day, often from nine in the morning, even on a Sunday. It was known as United's patch, so it was a big surprise that day when Forest arrived in the High Street with 250 lads.

You could not believe how happy everyone was when they came bowling down the road, as large as life. Everyone was piling into the road to take them on. It had been a lovely, sunny, tranquil morning and the idea of a mob turning up was not in anyone's mind, so when this mob popped up everyone clicked into gear. The only problem was that everyone wanted to get to them first.

If I was one of the Forest lads I would have done exactly what they did, which was to run. Kilburn High Road was now a mass of nutters charging towards them, praying for them to stand. They didn't. They turned and ran and were chased for what seemed like ages until the police arrived. No fighting, but that's what you got if you tried it on back then on cup final day.

We finally get to Crown Court in Manchester and when we arrive the police are not allowing anyone in the public gallery. Inside the court, they have a screen put up around the witness box to screen an officer who is due to give evidence in the case.

We are all in the dock. The judge comes in and does his nut. He demands to know who has authorised this. The prosecution say the officer must have anonymity. There then follows a week of legal argument. At one stage the judge has told the prosecution that if they do not comply with his instructions within fifteen minutes he will throw out the entire case. We're all laughing our heads off at this.

The trial ran into serious problems from the beginning. The police insisted that their undercover officers would only give evidence from behind screens to protect their identities. They claimed that allowing the officers to be seen could lead to reprisals against them from criminals watching from the public gallery. The defence argued strongly that having witnesses giving evidence from behind screen was prejudicial to their clients, because it gave a bad impression to the jury. In October 1991, Judge David Owen ordered the screens to be removed from Manchester Crown Court. He also threw out some of the conspiracy charges, saying that too much time had elapsed between some of the alleged incidents and the trial. The Director of Public Prosecutions responded by applying to the High Court to overturn the judge's two rulings.

In April 1992, the trial resumed, and prosecutor Rodney Klevan, QC, outlined the case. 'For a number of years, the violent behaviour of a small but significant number of those attending soccer matches has been giving cause for concern. The problems were not restricted to matters of crowd control inside football grounds, but extended to the behaviour of the so-called supporters before and after the games. On occasions violence occurred at times and places which apparently had no connection with football matches but [was] merely an attack on supporters of other clubs.

'By the late 1980s, the situation had got so bad that the term football supporter had become almost a term of abuse. In an attempt to combat the problem, the police stepped up their crowd control operation. Many more police officers were displayed at matches and used in various ways, simply as crowd stewards, as escorts to and from bus and railway stations, and in their traditional and visible roles as dog handlers and mounted police. Further innovations included the use of video cameras outside the ground. Video cameras had been used inside grounds with a good deal of success.

'However, as the violence became orchestrated and organised, conventional police methods became less successful and so further innovation was implemented. Specially trained under-cover police officers began posing as fans and made attempts to obtain evidence as to the people involved. You will not be surprised to hear that this was a dangerous task but the evidence obtained could not have been obtained easily by any other method.

'The evidence the Crown will call will include evidence from uniformed police officers, undercover officers, innocent civilians who were caught up in or affected by the violence, and some video recordings of some of the defendants mainly as identification evidence . . . We are concerned here with the activities of a group of Manchester United supporters. Although a number of the defendants are from Manchester, others live further afield. We will hear about "Cockney Reds" and "Barnsley Reds" – Reds, of course, because of the Manchester United colours.'

He went on to explain how the charges on the indictment included conspiracy – meaning agreement between two or more people to commit crime – and riot – where twelve or more people together use or threaten unlawful violence for a common purpose. '. . . You will hear detailed evidence of some twenty matches when observations were kept. As the evidence was collated, certain people were identified as being involved and were given "target" names. You will hear throughout names such as Alpha, Bravo, Hotel, but there is one name you will hear repeatedly. It is the Crown's case that the prime mover in this case is Kilo. Kilo is the target name given to O'Neill. It was to O'Neill the group looked for leadership and directions. If O'Neill wasn't present, others apparently took over – [November] apparently was in charge of the group during the incident in Newcastle.'

Yet the trial was halted once again in the on-going argument over the screens. The High Court said it had no jurisdiction over the matter of the screens and left it to the discretion of the judge. It did rule, however, that he was wrong to dismiss the conspiracy charges. The defence then appealed *that* decision to the House of Lords – and in May 1993, the Lords ruled that the High Court did not have the power to overturn Judge Owen's decision.

That shattered the case. Two and a half years after their arrest, the vast majority of the Operation Mars defendants – save for two who had pleaded guilty at an earlier stage to violent disorder – walked free. At almost exactly the same time, Manchester United won the Premiership for the first time in twenty-six years.

Tony O'Neill, however, had little to celebrate. He was in a hospital bed, fighting for his life.

Chapter Four

WELCOME TO HELL

AFTER THE COLLAPSE of Operation Mars, United's hooligan firm were ready to roll again. Manchester United were also about to embark on an unprecedented period of success that would, ironically, attract many of the Eighties' hooligans back. Alex Ferguson was making his mark, the glory days had arrived, and many who had deserted the terraces now resumed their Saturday afternoon antics.

One man who had arrived back on the scene with a bang was Paul Doyle. Born to a large family in the tough Lower Broughton area of Salford, Doyle was a lifelong criminal who committed his first burglary at the age of seven. He spent much of his youth in approved schools before hitting the pubs and clubs of Manchester in his late teens with the rest of his Salford crew. Doyle was a criminal and a very hard one at that; a fellow Salford gangster nicknamed him 'One-Punch' for his ability to flatten anybody with a single blow, a talent he demonstrated often.

His first Manchester United game – a trip to Newcastle at which he and twenty others were thrown out of the away end and had to fight hundreds of Geordies to get back to their coaches – was such a 'buzz' that he was hooked. Football violence for Doyle was 'fun', whereas crime was business. Sometimes the two combined: on his travels with United, Doyle saw how easy it was to raid jewellery stores in the confusion of a large crowd, to pickpocket and sneak thieve. He also learned about stolen credit cards and cheque books. In the mid-Eighties, he and some other rising Salford villains embarked on a spree of fraud and deception across Europe, using counterfeit bank notes, kiting cheques and spending bent 'plastic' to live it up and buy sackloads of designer clothes. Eventually busted by the Regional Crime Squad, they were charged with a range of offences including importing forged notes and conspiring to defraud the national clearing banks. Doyle was jailed for three years and five months.

At the end of the decade, Doyle was released from prison, and came out to the fast-growing rave scenes, which offered new and lucrative opportunities for those prepared to skirt the law. At the same time, he resumed his football trips. His first game back could not have been more volatile: Leeds United away. In one seventeen-day period, they played their hated Manchester rivals three times at Elland Road: on 29 December 1991 in the league (a draw), on January 8 in the League Cup (Man U won), and on January 15 in the FA Cup (Man U won again), and each game was marred by disorder.

PAUL: When I came out in 1990, I started to go to the football again with the lads I knew. They were Keith, whose nickname was Five-Star because he was always fancily dressed; Tet, who was 6ft 2in, overweight and a non-stop character who would dip your pocket within seconds, friend or foe; Jacko, who thought he was a porn star, with a pony tail; Ashy, another big lad, nicknamed the Jaw because when he was whizzing his jaw would be going non-stop; the Wing; Mark from Lincoln, another

6ft 2in, 19-stone kid who could fight for fun; and The Dot, who was there on every trip for us to take the piss out of, a straight member but last thing at night when he was drunk he would turn into the biggest villain ever. They were a real bunch of characters.

The first match I went to on my return was Leeds away. It was the period when we played them three times in three weeks. There was all new faces on the scene, including a mob called the Young Firm. We met in the pub and started walking down to Elland Road. The lads I was with were all saying, 'When it comes, nobody runs.' We walked further down and, bosh, it was upon us, Leeds coming from everywhere. I didn't budge and was immediately fighting so many lads in front of me. I had it in my head, don't run, because those words were the last I had heard from our lot, so I was going nowhere, even though there were loads of them.

Next thing, I hear, 'Get him down,' and I realise they are talking about me. I look round for support, only to see everybody else running away up the street. Never mind don't run, our lot were on their toes. I have to fight my way through Leeds, running the gauntlet of punches and kicks to catch up with the others, who now have a police escort.

The Leeds start shadowing the escort, trying to get in among us. Now, I had the capability of walking to the side of any man and whacking him with a snide. Not the most gentlemanly thing, but very effective. It is called side-stepping, and I can sidestep any man on the planet. I walked to the side of this big lump and side-stepped him and he went over. He had a big lumberjack shirt on and he was trying to get up but his legs had gone and the lads were all laughing at him.

A Leeds fan will put his charge sheet proudly on his bedroom wall to show he has been arrested against United. It's a badge of honour. On another occasion, we went to Leeds in cars and the police got on us. They said, 'You bunch are going to the ground with us.' I thought, *thank God for that!* We approached the Leeds part of the ground and the Leeds hoolies ran at us. The six coppers taking us to the ground ran off. Me and Mick Racey stood with our backs to the wall, fighting like hell. The Leeds riot police came running in and the Leeds fans ran off. I'm not going to run off with them so I got arrested – for having my back to the wall. As they were arresting me I saw Tet getting picked up off the deck, Godsell being picked up off the deck. It was carnage.

I got thrown in the back of the van with a load of Leeds and taken to a police station and put in a queue of fans being booked that was so big it went round in a semi-circle. We all had individual coppers next to us and even then the Leeds in the queue were singing, 'We hate Man U.' When they asked where I was from I had to whisper, 'Manchester,' which the copper then loudly repeated so everyone could hear it. In the cells they were singing, 'You Munich bastard.'

A couple of weeks after, three of our lads got hauled into the main police HQ at Chester House. The police said, 'We want to know what Paul Doyle is doing with you.'

They said, 'Look, we go back years with Paul, he's a good friend.'

'No,' said the copper, 'Paul is a different kettle of fish. He is more than a football hooligan.'

Their concern was justified. Paul Doyle was much more than a football yob. In the early Nineties, Manchester had become notorious not for hooliganism but for gang warfare. Factions from the city's Cheetham Hill and Moss Side districts had been involved in a long-running feud, then Moss Side's Alexandra

Park estate was split by a 'civil war' between two gangs. At the same time, big hitters from Salford were moving into Manchester's booming, post-rave clubland, taking over door security, running protection rackets and selling Ecstasy.

It was inevitable that the city's underworld would impact on the terraces. 'Grafters' and sneak thieves had been a part of the scene since the first forays away in the Seventies, and especially once the European trips began, while many of the worst villains were diehard fans of either City or United, with the latter historically drawing strong support from Salford. Paul Doyle became embroiled in a 'door war' that saw several people shot, and was also suspected by police of being involved in international crime. This would later have major implications on United's hooligan mob [see Chapter 7].

At the same time, the sudden prevalence of guns in the city, and people's readiness to use them, would almost cost Tony O'Neill his life. One night in April 1993, as he awaited the outcome of the Operation Mars trial, he was in a club called Ossie's in his home district of Wythenshawe when a fight broke out.

TONY: I was shot in a local dispute. I was in this club in south Manchester and there's a fallout. I'm at the back splitting it up and eventually a shotgun has gone off and I have been caught by the pellets in a ricochet. They penetrate my side and my arm. At the time it didn't hurt that much – it was 2 a.m. and a lot of beer had been consumed – and I thought it was no problem.

Only later, the yellow jaundice set in because some of the pellets had penetrated my liver and intestines. The actual injuries didn't seem that bad, but two days later, septicaemia set in. So for five and a half weeks I was in intensive care. I had five operations and eventually they stopped stitching me up and just kept clamps on me. This was in April, and what happens? United go and win the League. I heard about it as I lay in a hospital bed.

I'd be waiting all those years and they go and do that when I can't get there.

From what I later was told, the prosecutor said, 'If Kilo dies, the case will collapse.' They dropped the conspiracy against everyone at that.

That took me out of action for about half of the next season. I went down from about seventeen stone to under ten stone. And while I was away, the biggest firm the country had ever seen was running around, because we were trying to win the League. All that time I had been following United and I don't get to see them win the Championship. Instead I'm fighting for my life. I had five operations, and at one stage they didn't even bother sewing up my stomach because they knew they would have to keep going in there. Luckily because I was big I fought it off, but they don't know how.

In 1993, newly crowned as League Champions, United played Turkish side Galatasaray in the European Champions League. After a 3–3 draw in the Manchester leg, the team and supporters faced a harrowing trip to Istanbul that would pass into United folklore. The trip was marked by intense, almost hysterical hostility from the locals towards the visiting supporters. Even the United team was greeted at Istanbul's airport with banners proclaiming, 'Welcome to Hell.'

The night before the game, a mini-riot broke out at a hotel where many Reds were staying. The hotel was besieged by hundreds of baying Turks, while United fans inside were later blamed by the hotel management for trashing the bar and causing widespread damage. What has never been revealed is that the riot was sparked by the waving of an Israeli flag at the Muslim Turks by some of the United lads.

* * *

PAUL DOYLE: The best game I have been to was Galatasaray in 1993. A company called UF Tours ran the trip and took about 200 over in our group – twenty of us plus a lot of barmies – just ordinary, good lads. We get on this flight and UF have put someone on to make sure we behave ourselves. Tet was with us, buzzing away and lively. No-one could match him for the patter when he was on form; the only time I ever saw him get leathered verbally was by the comedian Foo-Foo Lamarr on a train once – Tet got slaughtered by him, but then the guy was a professional.

Now I'm half Jewish and have taken an Israeli flag to wind the Turks up. I'm planning to let Tet wear it on his shoulders because he won't know the significance, and it will be funny to see the reaction of locals.

Anyway, a guy comes out of the back of the plane absolutely bladdered, before we have even taken off. Tet puts his arm around him, gets him singing 'Ooh, aah, Cantona,' dips his wallet, takes his money and puts his wallet back.

Once in Turkey, they start to put people on coaches. We get a taxi instead and Tet is paying because he has lifted the money, but we go to the wrong hotel, so we have to walk to our hotel, which isn't far. Even as we were walking we felt like monkeys in a zoo. You don't see any women, everything is ninety miles an hour – and the locals were looking daggers at us. We even got spat at. I turned round and said, 'You dirty fucker,' and Tet is begging me not to do anything. You can feel the atmosphere just off Turkish straight members.

We get to the hotel. Everyone is at reception, handing in their passports but we go straight to our rooms, false names, etc, then decide to go for something to eat. We even take our cameras, like proper tourists. We sit down and for about 90p each had the biggest meal, beautiful.

Then I see two United fans run past being chased by thirty Turks.

I said to Tet, 'We've got to help.'

'Fuck 'em,' said Tet. 'They will just be barmies anyway.'

We finish, get to the ground and take some pictures. I have got a blond friend, Ashy, who is 6ft 2in. The game before, United goalie Peter Schmeichel had thrown a Turk off the pitch, and apparently the Turks had said that in revenge they were going to do Schmeichel in Istanbul. Some Turks were there and I pointed to one, pointed to Ashy and said, 'Peter Schmeichel.' A guy with a briefcase, look like a businessman, did not hesitate: he ran up and smashed Ashy in the face. Then he and five others chased Ashy into a taxi. My stomach was hurting with laughter.

We go back to the hotel. It's 7 p.m. We have just got back in Europe and no one has been to Turkey before and no one knows what it is like. No women in the city, and I hardly drink. *What are we going to do*, I'm thinking, *this is going to be so shit*. We hit a bar, ten of us. The rest of the 200 were all in different bars. I go to this little café bar that sells beer. Across the way we can see another twelve United at a different bar. The street starts to fill up with Turks staring at us. There was a couple of Turks in my café and one of them, every time Tet looked at him he said, 'What are you looking at, fat boy?'

I said, 'Tet, just throw a bottle on his head.'

But everyone has watched *Midnight Express* and is paranoid, so no one is throwing punches. The twelve from across the road come over and say, 'This is getting hairy.' It only needed one little thing to spark it off, and it wasn't long in coming. There was a girl with us and Massey from Rochdale has lifted up the girl's top and said, 'What would you do with them?'

All hell has broken loose. We had to pick up stools to stop them coming in to kill us. The police came with two minibuses and put us in. First time in my life I felt what a nonce would feel, because the Turks were howling outside and banging on the sides of the buses and trying to push them over.

They took us back to the hotel. Within half an hour, all 200 that went off drinking around the city had come back in covered in blood, all with a different story to tell. Some had been whipped back to the hotel by the police to get there faster than the Turks chasing them. We are all back by 9.30 p.m., thinking, *thank God we are home. We are safe.*

Then some of the United lads have attacked the bar staff and the hotel manager and they have all run out. It is now ours and we have a free bar. Me being the way I am, I think, *where's the safe?* One of the lads jumps over and gets the money. It's all notes in Turkish currency and looks like a fortune. We go to our room and share out the money, as you do – six or seven of us.

Ashy then said, 'Have you seen this outside?'

We are on the second floor and look out to the pavement, which at that part of the hotel is roughly at our eye level. There are literally hundreds of Turkish blokes on our level and about another 2,000 out in the street, being held back by the police.

I said, 'Right, get that Israel flag.'

We hung the flag out of the window like matadors waving a red rag at a bull. Every time I waved it there was a mad cry and all the Turks would charge down and try to get in the hotel. Those in the free bar were defending the door. Chairs, tables, pictures, everything. Meanwhile the Turks on the top level were trying to smash our windows in. Coco thought it was great and kept holding the flag out.

Every now and then this big group of United fans from Birmingham would run out at the Turks, would last two minutes and then you had to run out to drag them back in. Every one of them was full of blood. Then it was time to come on top – we knew the Turkish police would be moving in and arresting us all. We looked out of the window. Nobody had the nerve to jump out of the back window because it was the lions' den, but the choice was either get nicked and have your arse done in prison or go through that window. I did that window first and though I am not the quickest runner I did the fastest 300 yards you have ever seen. All the main lads got out and got into a different hotel.

Now, I can pass for a Turk or an Italian, especially with a suntan. So after a decent period, I snide back to the hotel to see what is happening. I wanted to be nosey. They are putting all the United in personnel carriers. I go to a kebab shop and order a kebab and of course they hear me speaking English and I end up being chased down the road by fifty of them and run into another hotel. They phone the dibble and I get arrested. I get fingerprinted at one police station, my photo taken at another and questioned at a third. They were looking for the people who had the money from the hotel, but that had long since gone down the back of the seats somewhere. All the Birmingham lads got charged because they were covered in blood, and the tour organiser got charged, but I didn't.

In the jail where we spent the night, there were black kids who hadn't eaten anything except bread for about four weeks. The toilet was a hole in the middle of the cell. It was like going back 3,000 years. The next day we sat outside the police station while they let one of our friends go for six kebabs. A normal guy came past where we were sat, walked up to us and slapped one of the lads three times across the face. Then said something to the copper, then went back and slapped him again. They hated us.

At 7 p.m., they put us on the coaches with tanks in front of us, all 200 crammed like sardines and 400 police, and took us near the airport. When we stopped, police lined both sides of the coaches. A kid took a picture of the police. They dragged him out, smashed his camera, gave him a hiding and put him back. When we got on the plane everyone was given their passports back and the pilot said, 'Well done to all those that have made it back. We just have to hang on for another two.' Tet and Massey were the only ones who made it to the game. Then the pilot said, 'Right, let's get out of this fucking country.' They had 'deported' stamped on their passports. It was hostile from the minute we landed. It was fantastic.

United's success on the field, and the attraction of exotic European trips, saw more elements of the old crew coming back together. The euphoria and friendliness of the rave scene was now wearing off and soccer violence was coming back into fashion among groups of thirtysomething males who had never quite got it out of their blood . They had known each other for years and now formed a tight-knit group that could not be infiltrated by any undercover officer or journalist. One of them was 'JB', who returned from a five-year stint on the other side of the world.

JB: I was a criminal as well as a football hooligan. I used to do credit cards and company cheque books. I went to the World Cup in 1986 with England, then I went to jail for fifteen months and after that I thought I had better shape up my life, and went to Australia in 1988. A lot of other lads did the same.

Just before I had gone away, my lot were losing interest anyway. They were more intent on gambling and boozing. United did have a firm of young tearaways who were really up for it and were aged around eighteen, while I was in my mid-thirties. We would have big battles with the Young Guvnors in town and City had a bit of an upper hand for a time, simply because a lot of their lads would hang about round town.

I was in Oz for five years, came back and they said that football violence had finished. Stadiums were all-seater, rival fans could walk out of grounds together at the same time, no bother. We went to Everton, seventeen of us, Doyley, Massey, Tet and the rest, in November 1993. In the past you took your life in your hands at matches like that but I thought this was lovely, a completely different atmosphere. We came out of the three-tier stand and normally you'd be on your toes, ready, but I was like I was on my holidays.

Then I heard, 'Here they are, here's the Munichs,' and there's about twenty of them waiting for us, led by Andy Nicholls. He came charging forward and it was just a toe to toe between their firm and ours that went on for a long time, backwards and forwards. That was the night Nicholls met One-Punch and got put on his arse.

That showed me it had not gone away, it had just gone down in size, from mobs of 4–500 to thirties and forties more intent on doing damage. Certainly there were no police there. For a good few years at Old Trafford they were letting away fans out at the same time, and maybe the police had gone to sleep a bit. There was a lot less in the mob when I came back from Oz but the faces were still there, like Tony. The young psychopaths had dispersed and it was the old firm again.

Chapter Five

FOOTBALL INTELLIGENCE

THE FAILURE OF Operation Mars forced Greater Manchester Police to adopt a different approach to their target hooligans. In keeping with other forces around the UK, they sought now to boost their intelligence gathering, in the hope of preventing fights, rather than try the now almost impossible task of infiltrating such clannish, tight-knit and suspicious groups.

The notion of long-term intelligence gathering, rather than relatively short but costly undercover operations, had been growing for some time. In the summer of 1988, England played in Germany in the European Championships. The tournament was marred by violence, with some United lads in the thick of the trouble. The Government decided a new kind of intelligence-gathering network was needed to prevent such scenes in future. In March 1990, the Home Office issued a circular to all chief officers advising them of the creation of the National Football Intelligence Unit, to provide a central point for collating, analysing and disseminating information about serious and persistent UK hooligans, to better co-ordinate police operations, to liaise with foreign police forces and to assess the extent and nature of 'football hooliganism and its criminal associations nationally'. It would also provide technical and some operational support with the use of 'optical evidence gathering equipment' – camcorders and cameras – and the analysis of video tapes. Though the NFIU was based in London, it was headed by a Manchester superintendent, Adrian Appleby. When United took a mob over to Italy in 1990, some of them were photographed and put on the new database, a computer imaging system called Picdar. The NFIU would eventually became part of the National Criminal Intelligence Service (NCIS).

At the same time, Greater Manchester Police was beefing up its own operation, and in time would have two full-time football intelligence officers covering United. One of them was PC Steve Barnes, a constable recruited from the drugs squad.

STEVE BARNES: Initially we had reactionary policing, hundreds of policemen but with no knowledge of who they were dealing with. When a fight started, they jumped in and hit people with sticks. What started off the notion of football intelligence was the Leeds riot at Birmingham in 1985, when the wall collapsed and horses charged across the pitch. That was looked on as a turning point. But it was very slow to begin with.

Greater Manchester Police made a public order film and they mentioned at the time there had to be closer liaison between clubs and the police and they were going to get together. Out of that came football liaison officers, but they were not intelligence officers. Over the next two or three years, around 1987–88, they gradually became intelligence officers, some part-time and some full-time. Then came the Hillsborough Disaster in 1989, and I guess everything took on a new urgency.

I had been working matches since 1978, and then became a part-time spotter about 1988–9. There was a process of going to one in four games and you would get to know names and faces and get more involved and I became very interested. Faces were my forte. In 1991, I went in the drugs squad for four years, then I joined the football intelligence office full-time.

There was no computer database at that stage. We had a small office at Stretford police station and Bob Betts was the intelligence officer. I came to form my own ideas about how it could be stopped, and eventually animosity grew between me and Bob. It got so bad that he stopped sending me to matches, so I did a report to the Chief Superintendent including my criticism of what was happening in the FI. I did Betts's legs, basically.

Hooliganism was becoming a serious problem again by about 1993. There were three distinct groups: the older Manchester lot, the young Mancs, and the Cockneys. The bulk of the mob at the time was actually the Cockney Reds. On a normal day there'd be possibly thirty or forty of the old Manchester lot and thirty or forty of the younger Manchester lot, but the Cockneys had seventy or eighty at every game. The older Mancs preferred to work on their own; they were hard lads and thought they stood more chance of a row if they walked away from the rest. There'd be O'Neill, Wing Commander, Doyle, Massey, Ashton, Harry the Dog. The younger Mancs didn't seem to have a leader but would often attach themselves to the Cockneys because the older lads didn't want them, apart from at the big games.

The Cockneys also had an older lot, led by Banana Bob, and a slightly younger lot who were very active. I was shocked that there was so many of them. The fight for them wasn't over when they left Manchester, it was going to happen at Euston and on the Tube as well.

————————

Intelligence on the Manchester contingent was initially harder to come by. They were streetwise and deeply suspicious of outsiders, and the existence of a strong criminal element within their ranks made them highly knowledgeable about police methods. Older, wiser and with plenty of disposable income, they would often stay in decent hotels for big trips, away from the main hordes, and do their own thing. Violence and bad behaviour, however, were never far away.

PAUL DOYLE: We'd stay at places like the Tower Bridge Hotel in London and we'd hammer the bar. One of the lads would phone, say, room 126 and say, 'Is Mr Davidson there?'

They would say, 'No, Mr Phillips.'

'Oh, sorry.'

Then we'd know the name of the occupant, so at night when it came to ordering drinks we would put it on the tab of 'Mr Phillips, room 126'. One time we were in the hotel nightclub drinking champagne and we all put it on the tab of a German guy who'd been drinking with us. The bill was about £1,800.

We played Villa in the League Cup final in 1994 and stayed in the Britannia Hotel in Docklands. We all got in the nightclub, where some of us are standing about because we're too ugly to pull. You have to come in this place smartly dressed, but twelve Millwall came walking in in shorts and summer gear, and the doormen were too scared to knock them back. These Millwall are taking liberties. The lights come on and the police are kicking them out because the doormen have called them.

Wing goes up to one of them and says, 'Listen, if you want it get 400 yards down the road away from the police and we'll have it.'

'Who the fuck are you?' says the Cockney.

'Forget who I am,' says Wing, 'we'll see you down the road.'

Six minutes later they are still there and this time another of our group has words with them. Then they move past us to walk outside. We have waited too long, and one of them, a bald-headed guy, gets a Budweiser bottle on his head. It goes off and it's fifty-fifty. They start shouting, 'Get the northern bastards,' to get the rest of the club to join in against us. Two hundred police arrive. Us football hooligans know when to throw punches and when not to, so we cool it in the foyer.

Outside, we see Tet being run round the car park by a 6ft 4in black lad and he's shouting, 'Doyley, Doyley, help me!'

'Fuck off Tet, you're on your own.'

The following year we played Everton in the FA Cup final and stayed at the Britannia again. We'd normally pick a hotel with a nightclub attached because forty of you can't get in a club in London otherwise. We get there, me and the normal good twenty, and we have invited a family of top Manchester gangsters to come with us. We walk in this club with them and seven or eight Scousers are in the foyer. They have come down in Bentleys and are all proper big-time gangsters themselves. The Manchester gangsters we were with were saying, 'Please lads, leave them, we know them.'

Then Mark from Lincoln had to say, 'Fucking gangsters, fucking sick of them.' The football hooligans didn't give a shit about gangsters.

It could have kicked it all off, but in the end we let these gangsters off, and they were having the night with us. But boys will be boys. Last thing at night, one of the Scousers was totally bladdered on the top floor of the hotel. Somebody saw him, robbed him, shoved paper up his pants, then set him on fire.

TONY: Unlike Forest a couple of years earlier, Villa didn't turn up at our drinking dens in Kilburn, but a lot of their lads were further down the line on the Tube. Myself and a few other lads had wandered off to some location away from Kilburn for some of our own skulduggery and just happened to walk into a full-blown scrap between United and Villa inside the Tube station.

Well, straight away the can of beer has been dispatched from my hands and lands on some Villa cunt's head, and we're into them from our direction. The tables turned in United's favour as they were holding off Villa from behind the barriers, stopping them coming over. Now United started coming over, as they could see we needed help before we were overrun. The noise was deafening in the confines of the Tube entrance and everyone was now punching each other as we were so closely packed together.

It never ceases to amaze me what goes on or what you see. For instance, you see a fire extinguisher landing on someone's head. Some people are swinging poles and brushes in the air, crashing on top of skulls. To be truthful it's fucking great, it's got everything. You can't beat that thrill; it's overwhelming.

And that's just what we did to Villa – overwhelm them. Eventually they were on their toes but fair play to them, they gave as good as they got. But they had one huge problem: they still had to get to Wembley on the Tube, and it wasn't over for them by a long way. It was like *The Warriors* trying to head back to Coney Island with a gang waiting at every stop.

They tried to get on another train but ran into another large firm of United who had already occupied the carriages. Villa's lads were on the platform and giving out abuse to straight members when this train pulled in. The doors opened and Villa were given a pasting. It was only the police that eventually got them to Wembley Way, and what a sorry bunch they looked. All United's lads were there on the approach, waiting to see if they could have another go. Not a chance; Villa's lads were done in and not a murmur was heard from them as they walked up. They were not even in a mob, just strolling up as though they didn't know each other. A bad day for them all round.

Another final in 1994 was against Chelsea, when United won 4–0. As usual we were all in London on Friday night – train, hotel, out, the usual routine for the FA Cup. The Friday night is usually great because everybody is there, anything can happen and usually does. The bar gets turned over, champagne, beer, the till goes west with all the money destined for our back pockets, any food or drink legitimately purchased goes on someone's room number, which you have assigned early on by hanging around about at reception looking for a name and number. Occasionally you would become the victim yourself, to everyone else's delight.

Saturday morning, nine o'clock, everybody was up. We were going to Kilburn early, as was most of United's firm, as Chelsea were obliged to come and take us on. Ten o'clock and Kilburn was full of United all down the High Road. Some of the pubs were already full as the back doors had been opened by friendly landlords. By eleven the lads are waiting and all are surprised that nothing has happened, though this keeps us on our toes.

We were led to believe a Chelsea firm was coming, so had thought they'd arrive early, but they didn't. We were led to believe they were going to sort us out as they felt they were the top dogs but maybe they didn't fancy it as they didn't have enough early on.

One o'clock comes and they arrive – about 5–600 of them, coming down the road, full of it. Must have been six or seven boozers filled with us so work it out. The problem is they are surrounded by police. The amount of uniformed officers was unbelievable. Imagine the scene as they come nearer: the whole High Road is full of United going towards them, egging them on to fight. I and most of the lads know nothing is going to happen as the police block off the road with vans and horses before they arrive and all that happens is two huge mobs are kept apart and Chelsea are herded back the way they had come. A total anti-climax, another day of bullshit, which happens regularly when some people think they can act like hooligans with mobile phones. The amount of times this happened was a joke, and with Chelsea it happened a lot. They don't like committing themselves to the unexpected, especially with United, but that's what it's about.

I saw no fighting that day but got reports of United fans being twatted as they strolled to and from the ground, fans who weren't looking for a fight. Call yourselves football hoolies? More like sad bullying twats.

The one fight where some Chelsea copped it was just past the top of Wembley way near the toilets, where some Chelsea were giving it the mouth and trying to take liberties. Some of the lads avoided the attentions of the police, came around from the food and toilet area and steamed into them, giving out a few good digs and backing them right off until the police intervened. I think the reason no major disturbances happened was because it rained bucketloads and everyone wanted to hurry out of it. Knowing Chelsea though, they will claim 100 of them ran 2,000 United back up the M1, or is that West Ham, because they were probably hanging about somewhere. I'm waiting for one of them to write a book entitled *We've Never Run*.

PAUL DOYLE: At Kilburn for the Chelsea game, some of the lads still had the hotel slippers on because they had got off so quickly without paying their bills. Kick-off was 3 p.m. but everyone was there early. Then two Chelsea lads came walking down. Wing likes to talk to them, being nice and all that. I go over and say, 'What's going on?'

Wing says, 'I'm telling them where to go if they want it.'

'Give them this message,' I said to one of the Chelsea lads. 'They are going to get worse than you.' And I broke his nose.

Ten minutes later, hundreds of them tried to run down this street at United, but the police prevented them.

This was the only game where we were forty-handed walking

down Wembley Way. When we go to a match, anyone with a shirt or scarf on can sit next to us and talk about the match. If they come with no scarf, wearing designer clothing, they are going to get a hiding. But on that day the Chelsea were beating up our barmies. We had to walk down Wembley Way turning every thirty seconds but we never lost one battle that day, while the Cockneys were knocking out fathers with kids.

After the match we got together outside Wembley. Mark is at the back and I'm at the front. Chelsea come to the front and the back at the same time. There was a black lad who had 'Chelsea' written on the back of his neck, it was that wide. I stepped to the side like a good little boy and boshed him and he was out. At the same time Mark knocked out another Chelsea fan at the back. They got done either way and had to run down Wembley Way. Our undercover officer later said to us that at the next game against Chelsea there was the biggest black lad you have ever seen walking around saying, 'Where's One-Punch Doyley?' He was fuming.

STEVE BARNES: When I first went in the football office, we had thirty or forty silly photos on the board and no names. I ended up with 400 pictures on a wall. My idea was that if I knew them and they knew I knew them, some deterrence was there already when they saw me on a match day. I had photos and CRO [criminal record] numbers and addresses. So when officers came in who were working games they could look at the board; I wanted everyone to know who was who. We eventually had a very impressive rogues' gallery, and even put roller blinds above the boards so we could pull the blinds over the pictures when we had people in the office who we didn't want to see them.

I was a spotter for three or four years and learned the trade. I saw what Bob Betts did and got to know names and faces and they got to know me. I realised the last thing they wanted was to get arrested, but some of them obviously thought they could fight in front of Bob and get away with it. I thought we should have been more active in prevention.

Betts was moved eventually to be an area bobby in Partington. So now there was me and a guy called Dick Giddings. We were the football intelligence officers (FIOs). Then Kieran Murray came about ten months after me and replaced Dick. He had been my partner in the Trafford M Division drugs unit and I classed him as a friend. The first game I did as an FIO was January 1995, a cup game at Sheffield United. Our base was in Stretford in the Sporting Events office. It was fantastic. I'd thought the drugs squad was great but this was a dream job. I had to pinch myself every day. I worked late, unpaid hours so that I got to know who everyone was. Then I set about getting informants.

One of the main Cockneys was widely believed to be into cocaine distribution. He was a wideboy and always gave the impression that he had a high lifestyle. When I first took over from Bob Betts, I'm sure this particular guy was testing me out. We were at Norwich and he walked up to a Norwich fan and started threatening him, right in front of me. He had obviously been able to get away with that in the past and thought he could do it now. I ran up to him, grabbed him by the neck, slammed him into a wall and shouted, 'What the fuck do you think you're doing? Don't you ever do that in front of me again.' He got the message. I was dying for the Norwich fan to punch him.

It was 1995, last game of the season at West Ham when we could have won the league but Blackburn won it instead, that 250 of United's firm met in a hotel beside Euston Station. Out of that 250, I would say seventy were Manchester lads. It was a good operation because we had an observation point at the station watching them arrive, and when they came out and went to the hotel we corralled them in, because about 180 Leeds were also in town, plus 120 Middlesbrough, plus Cockney gangs roaming around.

The Met corralled United against a fence as they came out of the hotel and videoed every single one, and that became our Bible of United's mob for years. I felt great that day because although we had got a lot of intelligence about who was who, we found out who talked to who and built up a pattern.

We started to get requests from the crime squads then about some of our targets, because they were involved in crime as well as football, and it did my credibility as an FIO a world of good, because I now knew a lot of them. I'd go in there chatting and they'd ask me why I was talking to them and I'd say, 'So I get to know you all.'

There was also a camera on the steps of Old Trafford, and where they used to meet on the forecourt I had a cameraman film them every game. Every Monday we would go to a video studio and freeze-frame and print off shots of their faces, so if there were any I didn't know I could go to the informant and find out who they were. Then at the next match I might go up to them and say, 'Hello John,' or whoever and they would jump in surprise because they had no idea that I knew their names.

I inherited Bob Betts's informant, who was not that good. I was determined to get a good informant in each of the three main groups at United. The first breakthrough came because I had a good relationship with the CO11 public order unit at New Scotland Yard in London, where the inspector was Barry Norman, a great guy. CO11 was also the force football intelligence office. They were top-notch, constantly asking us stuff and really responding. I dealt with them a lot because we were unique as a northern football club in having a large southern-based mob who were fighting other mobs on non-match days.

The Cockney Reds were not liked in London but they could hold their own and could turn out big numbers.

CO11 had an informant in the Cockney Reds and he proved useful. Then one of the young Mancs was arrested at a match. I spoke to him and basically blackmailed him. I said he was going to be charged and locked up but if he co-operated I would drop the charges. He didn't want to get locked up and tarred as a hooligan. I said, 'I don't want names, just where the group is and what the plans are. I want to be able to ring you on your mobile.' He agreed, and he was very good for about two years.

I eventually had 600 photos in my file and four informants: two in the Cockneys, one in the old Mancs and one in the young Mancs. I thought we had it made for the next four years and we were successful but the hard part was keeping it a secret. One informant was the best of them all. He was on £600 a month before bonuses and was probably the highest paid football informant in the country. CO11 called him the best football intelligence informant they had ever had.

We had different levels of intelligence, graded according to how good we thought it was. A1 was from a source who had always been spot-on in the past. The grading went right down to X4. X is not necessarily the worst information but is of unknown quality; it wasn't tried and tested. Someone might ring up a policeman and say, 'I was in the toilets of the Bulls Head and I overheard one guy telling another about a big fight planned for tomorrow night.' We would regard something like that as C2. If we then got separate, independent information that backed that up, we would upgrade it and send a summary down to whatever force area we were due to visit. Depending on how good they were they would act on it.

Of course, things didn't always work out the way we wanted. On one occasion, we had asked one of the main United lads to come into the office because we wanted to question him over an incident. We then tried to get into him to work for us as an informant. After a few minutes of us trying it on, we discovered that he had a tape recorder on him. I thought, *oh shit, this will now be played to all the lads*. But fair play, he said, 'It's okay, it's not switched on.' When we took him to the door to leave the building, there waiting for him was Tony O'Neill. He had apparently issued this guy with the recorder because he suspected what we would try to do.

It is only human nature that you like some people and dislike others. I didn't have much regard for a lot of the FI operations around the country. Tottenham were good; they had a very good guy doing it. Liverpool were pretty good and so was Arsenal, where Ray Whitworth was one of the intelligence officers. Ray was also the police security liaison for the England team and got to accompany them wherever they played. West Midlands Police just used to arrest people for very little and seemed to go out of their way to antagonise fans. The cells there used to be full, yet they never seemed to use or react to intelligence that well.

We would always travel to the away game. If it was over 100 miles we would go down the night before and stay overnight – and always have a curry, that was the rule! We would then liaise with the home cops. Ideally we would be in at the command briefing and stand up and give our briefing. That would take place at 8–8:30 a.m. Then there would be the intelligence briefing for the lower ranks, which we should be in on as well, then an intelligence briefing for the spotters. So there should be three briefings and that was the way we always did it, as long as it didn't impinge on the operation – for example if fans were arriving on an early train, you had to be out there doing your job rather than in briefings. But not all other forces did it.

At Derby County I arrived with good intelligence about a large mob of United arriving for a rumble and found their intelligence officer in the canteen giving out meal tickets at the same time as the Manchester train was coming in and our lot were spilling out on the streets intent on causing mayhem. It was crazy.

Chapter Six

CONTENDERS

DESPITE THE STRENGTH of United's football firm by the mid-Nineties, there were plenty of rival contenders for the unofficial title of Britain's worst hooligans. As in the Eighties, many of the bigger and more active gangs were at this time to be found outside the top divisions: in particular, the Soul Crew (Cardiff City), the Naughty Forty (Stoke City), and the Zulu Warriors (Birmingham City).

At the start of the 1994–5 season, Birmingham City were languishing in Division Two, two divisions below United, having been out of the top flight for eight years. Their multi-racial Zulu mob, however, characterised by their chant of 'Zulu, Zulu' as they steamed into battle, was undoubtedly one of the most feared around. And in September 1994, they saw an opportunity to attack what they imagined would be some of United's 'boys'.

A popular Salford boxer, Steve 'Viking' Foster, was due to fight Robert McCracken for the British Light-middleweight title at the National Exhibition Centre in Birmingham, on the undercard of a Nigel Benn world title defence. McCracken, a Brummie, was a Blues supporter and popular with the Zulus.

Foster, too, had a rowdy and extremely tough following drawn from the housing estates of Salford; like the boxer, they went by the name 'the Vikings' and had their own chant, taken from the movie of the same name starring Kirk Douglas and Tony Curtis. They were even known to launch burning cars into the Manchester Ship Canal to celebrate Foster's victories. Many were also diehard United fans.

It appears that the Zulus planned to return from their match that day at Oxford and ambush the northern lads inside the arena. The brutal brawl that followed was described as the worst riot ever seen at a British boxing match.

SALFORD VIKING: The Salford streets aren't paved with gold, they are paved with dogshit and last night's blood, but somewhere inside every kid from Salford there's a heart of gold. So when one of our own was fighting for the title, it saw the biggest mass exodus from Salford since the slum clearance. Over 1,100 went, all good lads on their day but on a bad day, fucking ruthless. Every gang was there: ram-raiders, gangsters, football hooligans, with one thing in common – they were from Salford.

Two or three coaches went from the Ashley Brook pub, a double-decker from the Weaste, others from the Woolpack in Salford Precinct, the Priory, which was the Vikings' den, the Church Inn, which was the older chaps, all pissheads but every one of them could fight; in fact virtually every pub in Salford had a representative heading down the M6 that night. There's always in Salford some kid who doesn't like another kid, but on that night when everybody came together, it was a formidable sight.

We got off the coaches at the NEC and most split up and headed into Birmingham. No-one was together because we had no inkling of any trouble to come. We got a taxi to some pub and there were quite a few of the Zulus in there and it was a bit on top, but we rode it out. They were telling us there was going to be trouble ahead and how no-one fucks about with the Zulus. There was only a few of us so we had to take it on the chin.

We made out way to the arena and when we got in there had already been trouble. A coachload of Nigel Benn supporters had had a bit of a kicking and a mob from Leeds had also had a spanking. The Zulus had all come in together and were mobbed up. They then attacked a Salford lot in the bar who were basically boxing buffs. The boxing buffs were no mugs and had a fight but they were heavily outnumbered.

When we arrived, we didn't know anything about this. Next there was a second fight and I'm sure it was the Ashley Brook mob from Liverpool Street in Salford. Same deal again, they were good lads but boxing fans, wouldn't look for trouble, and again it would be fair to say they were well outnumbered. I'm sure the Zulus did back them off but they hadn't yet met the Salford hardcore.

Then the fighting moved into the main arena. They started bullying people and beat up a couple of kids from Salford. The photographers went over taking pictures and the Zulus snatched their cameras. By this time, people from Salford were saying, 'Get together, get to our area and then we'll see what they've got.' The majority still weren't there; the Ordsall firm hadn't landed, the mob from Weaste had been stopped somewhere by police over a broken coach window, Cheetham Hill's mob was elsewhere and the Precinct mob were probably out robbing somewhere. No-one was together.

Salford were up in one corner of the arena in the upper tier. The Zulus came across the floor, through the temporary seating, to attack the main body of the Salford. They had plastic seats and metal brackets. That was the start of the third fight. It was a free-for-all and it was brutal. The stewards weren't worth a wank and just disappeared.

There were only about twenty Salford down at the bottom. These twenty, led by Mark Reddican, God rest his soul, took them on. Boom Boom was there at the front too throwing punches for fun and they stood there and held the vanguard, slugging it out toe-to-toe against much greater numbers.

Someone shouted, 'Please Salford, go back,' over the public address system, but they have now landed. They came over the top of the higher tier with one man in particular, Mad Dog, making his mark. Six foot five and with hands like manhole covers, he held a stairwell on his own, banging them for fun. Then the younger factions of the Woolpack mob – Gordy, Foxy, Laney – jumped over and started attacking from everywhere.

We will give Birmingham the first two battles because they were mobbed up and picked on boxing buffs. The third one, they can't deny because it was on television; Salford did them. When Don King came on television later, he said, 'I could hear the Viking song and I half expected Kirk Douglas to walk down the aisle.'

The police came but it carried on big time outside. We settled down to watch the boxing but now all of the Salford have finally arrived, and a lot were not very happy about missing the action. They wanted their two penn'orth. After the Foster fight had finished [he lost on points], the riot police were there, dog handlers, and the helicopter was that low outside you could almost touch it, but that didn't stop factions of Salford breaking through and chasing the Birmingham outside.

Some Salford kids ended up in Winson Green Prison and a couple of them got a bit of grief about one of the Zulu lads losing an eye. Mad Dog got a prison sentence, as did Mark Reddican. That night will be talked about for a long time.

Other 'contenders' coming up from the lower divisions relished the chance to have a go at United. Football fans like to have hate figures, and United's success on the field and perceived arrogance off it was rapidly making them the most despised club in Britain among other fans. Local rivals Bolton Wanderers were another side who had been outside the top division for a long time until their brief return in 1995–6.

TONY: We beat them 6–0 at their place in February 1996. Bolton were back in the top flight for the first time since 1980 and it was like the old days, as Bolton had decided that, no matter what, they were going to have it with United. From their point of view it didn't matter if you wanted a fight or not, you were going to get one, so on that day a lot of straight members took a whack, which is typical up and down the country. On the plus side, that sort of thing did the lads no harm, as it made it easier for us to get tickets. The straight members back then didn't go to as many games as they do now.

Before the game, there was open warfare on the streets leading to the ground and also around the stadium, which was a crumbling shithole. I was with about 100 lads, and as we got to the stadium, you could feel the hatred and also see up the street, where United's entrance was pure chaos, with people screaming and running about, all fighting each other. Quickly we got on our toes and got to the chaos and we started giving it to anyone who was there. A few headbutts were going in on the sly as the police were running around trying to quell the violence but it was going off all over. It seemed to me that Bolton had consumed so much beer they didn't care, so fists and boots were flying wherever you looked. All the police could do was drag United fans away towards the away end.

There were no arrests as the police had their hands full and everyone knew it.

Eventually we were in the ground and it was rocking on all sides as they spewed out all the usual Munich chants and abuse. This atmosphere was great, as each goal went in it got worse so the excitement and apprehension grew in us all, as we knew that no matter what the police did after the game, it was going off.

We were kept for five minutes in a pen at the back of the stand and were eager to get out onto the street, as we could hear Bolton going mad outside. There was the usual to-ing and fro-ing until eventually we got outside. Mayhem, that's what it was. As we tried to turn left away from the police, Bolton were bouncing around and we were quickly into them, knocking the first few over, but they weren't running away, so a mass brawl ensued right there in the middle of the street, with both sides knocking shit out of each other and blood spilt on both sides.

The fighting went on for a few minutes until we got down the road from the ground, and everyone was happy, with no-one nicked. The downside was that several United fans who didn't want to know, shirters and scarfers, were brutalised away from the main action. But if you were a United fan wearing such clobber, then unfortunately you risked it. These assaults on straight members were always going to happen, but ninety per cent of the time if we were there they had a chance of going unmolested. Unfortunately a lot of so-called hoolies get their kicks this way and think they're hard men.

On 5 May 1996, Manchester United played at Middlesbrough. It was the last game of season, and they would celebrate winning the Premiership once more. Like Bolton, they were fresh in the

Premier League. Like the Zulus, their Frontline firm was recognised as one of the most formidable in the country. Impregnable at home for years, they had spread terror among the lower divisions and were another squad itching to attack United.

Wild fighting after the match would be remembered by police and thugs alike for one stunning punch, thrown by the man known as One-Punch.

PAUL DOYLE: We all decided to go on a coach. The police are on us. They pulled the coach two miles from the ground and said anybody without tickets can't go any further. But we had a Boro season ticket book. Although the tickets are for different matches we dish them all out and the cops don't check the numbers, just glance at the tickets. So we all jibbed it to the ground, but the cops sent our coach back to Manchester.

We saw the game, then came out and it was hectic. What can we do? Our coach has gone so we have to get the train. As we are walking down, there are about forty of us and Boro are on both sides of the road. Even our undercovers have got their truncheons out and they are fighting like anything. It was like the 300 Spartans; we had nowhere to run. You couldn't get off.

We had fantastic fun. We are walking towards two buses. The police have surrounded us. The police walked on the other side of the buses because the Boro fans were on that side. But two of their main lads were twenty yards in front on our side. So I ran towards them and side-stepped one. Bosh. He was gone straight away. I punched the other and they were both gone. Half an hour later when we got to the train station and had to go in, the Boro fans applauded.

STEVE BARNES: Paul Doyle punching this guy was something else. I don't think I have ever seen anything quite like it, before or since.

Middlesbrough is a bad place to go because the new stadium is out among industrial estates and it was all bricks and soil and only one road in and out. You have to run the gauntlet of three or four pubs down this road.

You had the two mobs eyeing each other up outside after the game and we were in the middle. As we approached a double-decker bus, there was a tall Boro guy constantly giving it verbal. As they split either side of the bus, gobby made the mistake of going to the right with the United lot, while his mates went to the left. He was right by the bus window when Doyle went over and smacked him. It was an awesome punch. His head hit the window and smashed the glass and he went out like a light.

This mounted officer from Boro saw this and tried to get Doyle but he ran against the crowd, taking off his jacket to change his appearance. I've never seen him run so fast. We were laughing like mad. Kieran and I could have arrested him for what we saw but this guy so needed to be punched.

JB: I was outside the ground early and Boro were smashing any United all over the place, but then the gates opened at United's end and all the celebrating fans poured out, as we had won the league. Straight away I recognise all our lads and we get together and we are having it all the way back to the town centre.

About fifty of us set off walking and straight away they have clocked us on both sides of the road. We are loving it. It was on top, then it kicks. This guy looked like he had been hit by Tyson when Doyle smacked him into the side of the bus.

They come running in from behind, from the side, people are getting dropped. I get punched and dropped, get up, punch someone myself and he goes down an embankment. Then I get chinned from behind and I'm on my hands and knees. Then there are some arms around me and I saw the radio in the inside pocket and realised it was a copper. I thought I was nicked, but instead he said, 'Fuck off now Joe, it's on top.' In truth he saved me from a kicking.

Then Middlesbrough have made a big charge right into us and Steve and Kieran have shit it, truncheons drawn but they are going to get swamped. Steve looked at me in horror but now it was my turn.

'Don't worry,' I said. 'We're having this.'

And he and his mate have taken a back seat then and we have gone for it big. It takes fifteen minutes to walk and it was some of the best fighting I have ever seen in my life. No one winning, no one losing. You get to the town centre and it narrows to get to the railway station and there are Boro everywhere. Police are surrounding us by now. I will never forget what happened next. I heard applause, clapping, and thought, the piss-taking bastards. Loads of Boro were beside us and I said to a copper, 'Why are they taking the piss?' and he said, 'They're not, they're applauding you.'

One of their lads said, 'We have never had a firm do that before.'

We had black eyes, broken noses, but the journey back was superb. It was like the tales from Europe.

TONY: The next time we played Boro at home, their boys were coming down on the train and were phoning up a certain United face on the way, saying, 'We are coming,' etc. So the United lad told them, 'We will stay offside and will tell you where to go when you get off.' So we stayed where we were, but five minutes before they got off the train, they turn off the phone. Then we heard they had all come down the approach and gone in the first pub, the Waldorf. We had one or two lads around the station. United all came through the side streets and charged across. Boro were outside and in the doorway but wouldn't come out. There were only three coppers there, so a couple of Boro were whacked in the doorway before more cops turned up and we got off. But we couldn't understand why the Boro had turned off their phone.

Chapter Seven

GANGCHESTER UNITED

THE CRIMINAL SUBSET within United's firm was about to get bigger. The catalyst was Paul Doyle, who around this time was involved with a major European crime gang. Police believed their activities included, among other things, the smuggling of large amounts of contraband. A pivotal moment occurred with what became known as 'the rip'. The European firm were apparently taken for several hundred thousand pounds' worth of cannabis – which the Salford contingent then refused to pay for. The criminal Mr Bigs blamed Doyle and his partner, Graham Boardman. They threatened to kill them both if the money was not paid – but it wasn't.

What happened next has passed into underworld legend. Boardman was lured to Spain under the offer of another drug deal, then apparently abducted by a large number of heavily built men. It is believed that he was then tortured to death; his body has never been found.

According to the crime cartel, Doyle was next. With a death threat hanging over his head, he faced a dilemma. Many of his associates among the Manchester crime fraternity had dealings with the same European gang – and were in a position to betray him, for the right price. So he turned for back-up not to the underworld but to the people he could trust: the football hooligans.

PAUL DOYLE: I'd had a reputation as One-Punch Doyley since me and Paul Massey hit Manchester in the early Eighties, when I was twenty-one. We are talking about the city which is the Chicago of England, and I made my mark. By the mid-Nineties I was involved in a top, organised European firm whose base was Puerto Banus on the Spanish coast. The Yugoslav Mafia was involved and the main lads on the Costa del Crime. Football was just my pleasure. We were all lads in our thirties and each one of us had that nagging wife and we could say to them we are going out to the football match and we are coming back at 3 a.m. and as far as the wives are concerned we are travelling all day.

Then one of my partners gets killed. The situation I had was, who do I turn to? Do I go in hiding or do I turn to the Manchester gangsters I know, each of whom could be bought?

I realise that the people I can turn to are those I know best, and what I had around me was the football hooligans, who don't know gangsters. They live in different worlds. You can talk about Manchester Mr Bigs, but the football hooligans didn't give a fuck about Mr Bigs. When you hit nightclubs, gangster or no gangster, nobody takes guns in, so if anything happens it's not down to shooters, it's down to whatever weapon comes to hand, and the hooligans were as good at that as anybody. In Manchester at one stage the police put up roadblocks at weekends to search for guns and knives, but the most common weapon was the Budweiser bottle, and sometimes at night we'd have seventy guys in Henry's armed with these bottles. I couldn't put a figure on how many fights I have had because we are professional fighters. We can have 100 lads running at us but we know we'll stay there.

So if any hired Scousers came for me, sent by the Puerto

Banus crew, they will have seen me with seventy lads there and they have got no chance; any Cockneys, the same story. Openly I'm standing solid with the biggest firm in Manchester. A Division had us higher up on the board than any proper known villainy firm. And the lads were 100 per cent strong behind me.

And no firm could cross us. When I first met them, a lot of these were nine-to-five workers, married. Half of them got divorced the first year and every one of them gave up their jobs. And that's how a group of our hooligans became gangsters.

Yet even surrounded by his football firm, Doyle was a target. In April 1997, a large contingent of United lads travelled to Amsterdam for some recreation before heading to Dortmund in Germany for a European Champions League semi-final. Amsterdam, as well as being one of Europe's most beautiful cities, is a centre for international organised crime, in particular drug trafficking. The cartel that Paul Doyle had upset had many influential contacts in the city, and by going there he was putting his life in grave danger.

PAUL DOYLE: Our plan was to hit Amsterdam and then go to Dortmund. Forty of us got a flight. Some of the people on the trip, gangsters, were working with the Puerto Banus lot at the time, while a couple of others who should have come on the trip cancelled. I have still got problems with people wanting to kill me, and when I go to Amsterdam, I am walking into the Devil's den. As long as you are not Dutch the police there are not bothered.

At the airport, me and Ashy are told we are not welcome in Amsterdam and are ordered to sit with fourteen United fans waiting for the plane back, but we wait until their backs are turned and jib through Schiphol Airport in the mayhem.

We are in Amsterdam and the night comes. Fifty of us are in this bar and I'm sat on the pool table, half-drunk and bored. Then a kid comes over, being loud, a 6ft 4in Dutch cloggy.

I said, 'Who the fuck are you, mate?'

'I'm number one Ajax hooligan.'

'Is that right? Meet number one Manchester United hooligan.'

I picked up the pool cue and hit him over the head with it. Then he grabbed the other end of the cue, and me and Ajax's number one thug are having a tug-of-war with the cue. Eventually I said, 'Keep the pool cue,' and went in with my fists.

Then it all kicks off. The doormen come in but get bombarded with pots and bottles and are in a mess in seconds. Then I said, 'Split up lads and get back to the hotel.' We knew the police would be along.

We leave the bar. I'm with Wing and his brother and one of the gangsters involved with the Puerto Banus lot. Down a little alleyway I see a police motorbike turning in. I had a black leather coat on and knew they would be after the one who started the fight, so I gave it to Wing's brother and said, 'They'll be looking for me, you wear the coat and sit over there.'

We get to another bar. The police come walking in with one of the doormen from the fight and point straight away at Wing's brother and arrest him and put him a van. We all had our hands checked and then were told to go, but as we reach the door one of the other doormen realises they have got the wrong guy. We leg it to the hotel before they can catch us.

I say to everybody, 'Look, they are going to ask him what hotel he is in and they are going to come back and arrest everybody. So we need to split for a while.' The others are saying. 'You're paranoid.' One hundred per cent I was paranoid. I'm a villain and I know how the police work.

Anyway, at 1 a.m. I am back in the room I am sharing with a lad called Beb. I get a phone call.

'Hello,' in a Dutch voice. 'Is Paul Doyle there?'

I think it's the Dutch police. 'He's not here,' I reply. 'I've changed rooms with him but I'll go and get him. Give me five minutes.'

I get my boots on, go down the fire escape and disappear into the red light area. I meet two of my other friends, Keith and Timo. 'I think the dibble are at the hotel,' I tell them. They were in one of the brass gaffs and I couldn't get them out for an hour so I have to wait around until they have both finished.

On our way back the police have obviously been told to pull any English they see. They see us and shout at us to stop but we run back to the hotel again. I go back to the room and see Beb.

'There is a black kid that has just come to visit, left his name and said he will be back in an hour,' says Beb.

Now it all falls into place. I know who this black lad is, he's a Dutch kid who runs all the black mob over there. He is also one of the ones that wanted to whack me out for the Puerto Banus lot. He has been tipped off that I'm in Amsterdam, at that hotel, and he's trying to find me to have me rubbed out.

I thought, *fuck this, get everybody up* – except the Manchester gangsters, because I knew I was betrayed either by them or by others who had not made the trip. So I got all the football lads up in the foyer. We couldn't buy drinks by this time, all we could get was coffee or tea.

An hour passed and another black lad came walking in, trying to look casual. One of our lads approached him straight away and said, 'Are you looking for somebody?'

He saw how many were there and said, 'No, I've just come to use the phone.'

'The phone's there,' said our lad.

The black lad looked around again nervously and said, 'No, too many, I'll use another phone.' Then he left. If he'd pulled a gun he'd have been the first person ever bombarded to death with cups of coffee.

Then a message came to the foyer for me from the Puerto Banus lot, saying, 'We always know where you are. We will be seeing you again.' It was the fight in the bar that had saved me by making me paranoid.

Next day we went to Dortmund. The Puerto Banus influence did not extend to Germany, so I could relax. Instead we had some proper hand-to-hand fighting. A big German comes running in to us, doesn't get knocked out but takes loads of punches, then runs off twenty seconds later. If they did what the English do and all came in together they would never lose. I chased one that same match and he was about 6ft 6in. I kicked him in the leg and it was like kicking a tree. I was thinking, *why is he running? He's massive.*

Then we were at the ground and two coaches of what looked like the army pulled up and started to get off. I said to one of my friends, 'Fuck this, I'm off.' Because there was fifty of us in a group and we were the obvious target. Sure enough, as I got off the army surrounded the fifty and took them all away. They had to watch the match on a big screen.

––––––––––––––––

The gangster connection would become a big part of United's firm, and of its mystique. Other mobs began to hear stories of 'the Salford mob', and it began to have a psychological effect. Fighting fellow hooligans was one thing, but facing vicious, hardened criminals on the streets was something else entirely. Though they wouldn't admit it, few rival mobs really fancied taking on the United hardcore, the big men in their late thirties with hard stares, bottle scars and prison tattoos. Another factor that enhanced this image was their adoption of all-black clothing, something they would later become noted for.

* * *

PAUL DOYLE: We used to all dress in black because when we went out on a Saturday morning, a match day, we were not getting back until 4 a.m. Manchester at this time was full of fancy wine bars, often where the players themselves went, and you couldn't get in them in jeans or whatever people used to wear for the match. You would get in, though, in black jackets and jumpers, so people started wearing that to the match and going straight out afterwards for the night. Hence the Men in Black, but that's all there was to it.

We became very well known on the Manchester nightlife scene. We had ninety per cent of the clubs boxed off; we could just walk in with no queuing. People said it was like the film *Goodfellas*, but they had to get in through the back door; we went through the front and the queue had to step to one side. All the Manchester gangsters knew they couldn't fuck with us but they weren't bothered because half the hooligans were straight members, so they weren't part of the underworld anyway.

The two main clubs were Kells and Peruvia. In these clubs the hooligan world and the gangster world would come together, and sometimes they would come into conflict. One of the football hooligans was Smiley Bri, who was called that because he always had a cheery grin on his kite when he had a fight. On one occasion in Peruvia, a top-rank United player was in there with a friend. Well, his friend was being a bit loud in front of Smiley Bri, who ended up knocking him out. Then the football player went over to one of the high-up members of the Gooch Close gang from Moss Side. Very dangerous people. The Gooch lad comes over to sort it out and Smiley Bri knocks him out.

Now this is a serious situation, a gang head getting decked by someone in a club. People have been badly hurt or even killed for less. Sunday morning comes, I get a phone call from someone who I'll call G, who is very influential with the black gangs.

'Paul, what happened last night?'

'What do you mean?'

'X got knocked out by one of your mates.'

'Give me five minutes, let me phone about and find out what has happened.'

I make a few calls, then get back on the phone to G. 'Looks like it's Smiley Bri,' I say. 'What are you going to do? Are you going to bring the guns out and risk one of the lads getting twenty years for a shooting because one of your mates can't take a punch? To come for this guy with guns is pathetic. Let common sense prevail.'

G said, 'My guy can't fight Smiley Bri one-on-one because he is too big. Bring the guy next Saturday, just you and him, he apologises and everything will be all right.'

'Right, no problem.'

Next Saturday we met in Courtneys. Paul Massey from Salford came with about thirty lads. Damian [Noonan, head doorman at the Hacienda nightclub] came with twenty-five lads. Various others. I had eighty of the football hooligans myself, the biggest convoy you have seen going to Peruvia. It was not a problem with G, who is a very, very good friend of mine, but everybody wanted to be in on the meet.

We walked into the VIP part, this army. G was there with fifteen of his lads – all gloved up. He turned round and said, 'Fuckin' hell Paul, I thought you were coming on your own?'

'I thought you were.'

Then I said, 'Look, we haven't brought the kid because if we did it might kick off. Let me buy you a bottle of champagne.'

He said, 'We are forgetting about it because this kid is not a gangster.'

And that was the end of it.

When I first went in Kells, it was because I had started to go out in Manchester and if I got up to go to the toilet, seventy lads got up with me. They were always watching my back but sometimes I need a rest from it. Kells was near Manchester Airport and I could go there to chill out. The first night I went there, on my own, the doormen were very nice: 'Look, Paul, you are very welcome here.' I stood with my back against the wall and enjoyed the night. Then they go and sack the doormen for letting me in. The week after, Ned Kelly, who ran the security for Manchester United, has taken over the door security. This time I take two or three friends with me. Now, ninety-nine per cent of the door lads I know anyway; I have been going out in town for twenty years. At the time, there wasn't a doorman who would knock me back, out of friendship. So we get in and I have a couple of drinks.

Ned comes over and says, 'Look Paul, we will let you in no trouble.' I was talking then to the owner – as I was going in I had seen the owner pull up in a Merc. We were up in the VIP part and chatting and I said, 'Listen, you got rid of some doormen for letting me in. If I ever get a knockback from this place, I'm not going to blame the doormen, I'm going to blame you.'

'Me?'

'Yes, you. And all I would do is wait for you to pull up in your Merc, take your number plate down, give it to a friend, he will give me your address and you might get a little visit off one of my friends.'

He was shocked that I knew he had a Merc. Of course it was all bullshit because I wouldn't go that far over not getting in a nightclub, but he folded.

'Do you want a drink Paul? Let it be champagne. You are welcome here any time you want.'

I then knew the place was mine. The week after, everyone now knows where I go and there are forty lads all in black, who'd all had a day at the match. The football players are in, all United's main stars. And that was how Kells became the base.

Kells saw the mob and the players rubbing shoulders. An exclusive club, its doormen were provided by Ned Kelly, the former SAS soldier whose SPS Security were responsible for stewarding and player safety at Old Trafford. It therefore attracted United stars who could enjoy a night out without being hassled. In this regard, being close to the gangsters could help, by deterring some of the more idiotic drunkards from misbehaving or trying to pick a fight with a footballer.

The mixing of professional footballers and gangland elements is not new. They often come from the same background, even the same estates, frequent the same bars and clubs, share the same leisure interests – gambling, clothes, women. Soon many of the United stars were on nodding terms with the heavy mob. Occasionally, however, the two would come into conflict.

PAUL: One night we had invited some lads down with our friend Mark from Lincoln to Kells. He has brought some diehard Reds. We go to the Four Seasons about 3 a.m. and some Manchester City players are in there and these kids go over to Terry Phelan and put a bottle of champagne over his head. Don't know why. It said in the *News of the World* 'smartly dressed thugs', so that is what wearing black does.

One time it was Andy Cole's birthday and he was with about forty lads. I'm with Greek George, he's 6ft 2in, eighteen stone, and Sully, who is also 6ft 2in. Cole goes to the toilet, comes out and Sully says, 'My mate here puts a one on you every week to score the first goal and you never do. You're shit.'

I jump in and say, 'Sully, leave him. They live in their world and we live in ours. Sorry mate.' And we go off.

At the end of the night, as everybody is getting off, Sully says to Andy Cole, 'Hey Andy, pass us the ball.'

Cole, who has had enough by now, says, 'What is your problem, you prick?'

'You're my problem,' says Sully. 'I love United and you're shit.'

Andy Cole whips off his jumper and says, 'Me and you, let's have it.' I had to jump in and the doormen came running up. Cole would have half-killed Sully. They are both shouting at each other, while Cole's friends are holding him back, saying, 'Andy, you're a footballer.'

He said, 'Not tonight I'm not.'

I said, 'Leave it out, we all drink in the same city.' Common sense prevailed.

The next game, Andy Cole scores three. I said to Sully, 'You should have done that six months earlier!'

Two months pass and we're on nodding terms with Cole. Then United sign Dwight Yorke and him and Cole are big mates. One of our friends is a leading professional who plays for another team and his wife is with us in Kells. She goes over to Yorke and says, 'You might know my husband.'

He says, 'How the fuck would I know your husband?'

She asks him who the hell he thinks he is and gets told to fuck off. She comes over to us and tells us what has happened. Then Andy Cole, who now knows all about us, has realised she is a friend of ours and comes over and asks if she will accept an apology.

I said, 'Why are you asking us? Ask her.' She got a bottle of champagne bought her.

We went from Kells to the Four Seasons hotel next door, where you can drink late. We go into the hotel and I'm talking to Ned Kelly and some of the footballers. There's a scuffle at the door. One of my friends called Mick, who can have a fight, was having a young kid a battle. We have gone to see what's happening, then everyone is saying, 'Leave it, man to man.' But it was my friend who was getting kicked in the head. I said, 'No.' I couldn't embarrass myself by jumping in on a young kid, but my friend was taking a good hiding. We stop the fight and take Mick into the toilet.

We find out why Mick was losing the fight. This nineteen-year-old has stabbed him in the neck twice with a bottle. The blood has been pouring out of him and he is all drained out. We came out of the toilets with him pumping blood.

The kid who did it was a young Stockport County footballer. Two other Stockport players there got a good hiding and I think Andy Cole would have said to Dwight Yorke, 'That's what you nearly got.' The next week, forty lads, all hooded up, went to Stockport County football ground on a training night, stopped the training, terrified the coaching staff and demanded, apparently, £20,000 in compensation from the club. And the kid who'd been involved in the fight got shelved by the club.

Even Beckham used to go to Kells. We have known him since he was a teenager; Mick had to front him in Courtneys on one occasion for messing about with one of Mick's birds. He used to hit the nightclubs by himself, make his own way to a club he knew we were going to. We would be in the far corner of the VIP part of Kells. There would be Ned and all the other players, while we would be there twenty-handed.

On one occasion Andy Cole was talking to my wife, who was telling him she had just got a rottweiler. Beckham said, 'I've got two rotts. You should get Paul to spit in one of their mouths and you in the other and then they know who is boss.'

Jeanette says, 'Are you telling me Posh spat in the other dog's mouth?'

'Yes.'

'Well that's not very posh, is it?'

On this occasion I was in there with Ned and the club was rammed. It must have been ninety-six degrees in there yet Eric Cantona was about ten yards away with a long mac on. Ned loved Cantona. I said to him, 'Ned, he has to be sweating his bollocks off.'

'Mister Cool never sweats,' said Ned.

A couple of minutes later, Eric comes back from the toilet and someone throws a tissue towards him. He instantly flinched back and covered up like it was a bottle. Maybe he thought it was, but so much for Mr Cool.

Sometimes some of the United players would throw questions at us. They were more intrigued about how we lived than we were about them. On another occasion we are with one or two players and leave Kells to go to the Four Seasons. There had been an incident a week before when a lad got a hiding and the blame had been put on us. The police had put in one of these oval light balls which was a £5,000 camera to watch us, and put metal bars over the video so no one could take the tapes out. On Mondays they'd go to the club and wanted to know everything that had gone on the previous weekend.

On this night I was walking behind all my lads from the club to the Four Seasons. I was talking to Beckham. Ten of my lads are outside and said, 'Paul, they're not letting us in.' They're all big lads and I'm only 5ft 9in, but they have been waiting for me to come along and sort them out. There were two doormen. One of the doormen turns round and said, 'Becks, Dave, leave it five minutes.'

I said, 'What's going on?'

'Paul, it is the doormen doing their job,' said someone.

'Fair enough,' I said. 'I'm doing my job.' Bosh. The gift from God came and the doorman was knocked out and the other doorman ran off past me. Then we went into the place. That was the last time we ever saw David Beckham.

I apologized that night and gave Ned Kelly a cookery set worth five grand that Sully had nicked the week before. I promised him there would not be any more trouble in the place. The week after we were back in. Well, we can't be controlled by the doormen, even though one of them is a world champion Thai boxer and it would be impossible to have a fight with him. We're like a pack of hyenas; we throw punches all at the same time. We go back twenty years and if it kicks off, one doesn't shout, 'I'm at the side of you.' Every one of them wants to be in front of you and in first.

I had taken an E and was chilling out leaning on the back door. Whenever I take an E I get paranoid to death. One lad comes over to me with a Scouser and says, 'Paul, I want to introduce you to this lad.'

I said, 'Hello, how do you do? What do you do for a living?'

He said, 'I'm a snide.'

I thought, *typical fucking Scouser*. I said, 'What do you mean, you're a snide?'

'No, I deal in snide clothing.'

'Well if you deal in snide clothing, say you deal in snide clothing. Don't say, "I'm a snide."'

'What I have come over for is I need a bit of money collecting.'

Now at the time I was on fantastic money. To be used as a debt collector, I had left that behind years ago. This was an insult.

I said, 'Mick, take your mate away.'

His mate went away. I was talking to one of my friends who was a top international rugby player for Ireland and said if it hadn't been for my promise to Ned I would have battered the Scouse prick all over the place.

Ten minutes later, my wife Jeanette is at the bar ordering a drink. Around the corner of the bar were two good-looking, wealthy Arabs. Most of the people in the VIP lounge are millionaires. I said to Jeanette, 'They've been chatting you up and you've been having it.'

She says, 'Fuck off Paul, give your head a wobble.'

'I'll give your head wobble.'

Jeanette throws a drink over me. We have a massive argument and all our friends jump in between us. Then she goes running out of the club.

I have made that much of a cunt of myself that it can't get any worse, so I think, where is that Scouser? I started throwing Budweiser bottles at him and he is running about the club like a headless chicken. Kells got shut down after that. They turned it into a gym and I ended up training there.

Things got out of hand. The police knew what we were about. On one Friday night we went to Leeds and 200 riot police were waiting for us. They started to stop us from going into cities.

We went to Lincoln, all the football group. On a previous occasion there, the police had surrounded our hotel and said, 'Either we escort you out of Lincoln in your cars or you stay in the hotel all night.' On this night there were twelve of us. As we walked down the street to a nightclub we could see all the CCTV cameras in the street turning towards us.

We got in the club but the last four in the foyer had to pay. Benny was one of them and he is a smart-talking lad, confident. We used to call him Benny Redband because when Strangeways was Strangeways and everyone hated the screws, he had a redband [trustee] job, which was unheard of. Benny is cute.

The foyer is camera'd up and the doormen are all big sted-heads [steroid takers]. There was a doorgirl there, and an argument broke out about Benny not getting in for free. This doorgirl lassoo'd him with some kind of dog handling device and choked Benny out. We are not going to be mongs and attack the doormen where the cameras are – we want them to come inside the club. But the doormen won't come in, so we go to the bar, order twenty drinks and then refuse to pay. So what the clever bastards did was let off the fire alarms so the police would come to clear the club. We can't do anything about it, but we don't forget.

One of my friends is a world champion boxer, another one

provides all the ringcard girls, so I have no problem getting boxing tickets. This night there's a big fight card on at the MEN Arena in Manchester and I have to go down and pick up my tickets. It's June or July and I'm in my friend's Ferrari. Deansgate is being dug up and traffic is not allowed down, but I have taken an E and I am going down it. There was a popular pub called J.W. Johnsons and on a sunny day everyone would hit the pavements outside there and the Moon Under Water.

It is 6.30 p.m. Cones are stopping people going down the road but I go round the cones, the only car on Deansgate, hammer this Ferrari down the rough tarmac and skid to a halt outside Johnsons. I get a big cheer off them all. We get the tickets and are all there.

When we went to football matches, sometimes we'd be followed by 200 lads because they knew that where we went, trouble would follow. They also used to find out where we were going at night and would turn up there too. So we get up to go to the boxing and 250 people stop drinking and follow us down the road.

You can get to the Arena through Victoria train station and there are only so many security on four different doors. This 250 hit the doors and do the security, no problem. It was the time gas had first come out. The police also had gas and ran up and gassed the mob, but they simply gassed the police back and had them running the other way. Everyone goes in and takes over the best seats in the house. The security can't do anything and the police say, 'Just let them sit there and watch the boxing.' But they are unhappy.

On the way out, the riot cops have come to Tony [O'Neill] and said, 'We are coming for you. What you have done is put the innocent Joe Bloggs at risk and we are not having it. We are going to come for you.'

Tony said, 'Let's have it now.'

The flag says it all. The dibble clearly believed I was the ringleader, so there was no point being shy about it.

MANCHESTER UNITED TAKE ON THE JOCKS

This picture was taken outside Hampden Park football ground last May during the Scotland -v- England match, and shows a number of Manchester United supporters who are just setting up a confrontation with rival Scottish fans just prior to kick-off. Note the chap with the red dot - he is our old friend Anthony O'NEILL, from 116 Gladeside Road, Wythenshawe, who is reckoned to be the organiser of a large gang who regularly support United both home and away. Since his arrest in March this year (case dismissed) he has taken a low profile during actual violence, but is still seen organising his troops at the Toll Gate Inn or in the City Centre. We are extremely interested in his activities/associates.

A Greater Manchester Police intelligence bulletin on me, prepared even before the start of Operation Mars, with a photograph taken at a Scotland v England game at Hampden Park.

Some of the lads had this banner made up to take a friend on day release from Full Sutton Prison, near York, to a United match in London. Far right is One-Punch Doyley.

The aftermath of a ferocious brawl at the Birmingham NEC when the Zulu Warriors came up against the Salford boys, who had gone to watch boxer Steve 'Viking' Foster fight for the British title. The result was called the worst riot ever at a British boxing match. © Caters

A trip to Leicester City saw the Men in Black come up against the Boys in Blue. Here I discuss the finer points of match-day policing with a baton-happy inspector. © Leicester Mercury

The police response: hit them with sticks. At the end of a bruising day, the inspector saw me off on the train with the words, 'See you next year, Tony' © Leicester Mercury

A trip to the Far East took in the famous Dog's Bollocks bar in Thailand, run by a couple of former Chelsea faces.

Another shot of the lads in Pattaya Beach. United's success in Europe led me to start my travel company and run trips abroad, not for hooligans, as the police insinuate, but for fans from all walks of life.

Big James, one of a number of Hibs lads who teamed up with United in the late Nineties, when some started calling us the 'Superfirm'.

Another match-day trip, this time to Athens, relaxing with some of my customers by the pool, just how it should be. This was the day New York's Twin Towers were attacked, and the match was cancelled in sympathy.

A sequence that shows the unfolding of part of the major confrontation between Leeds and Manchester United supporters on the Holbeck estate in Leeds. The photos speak for themselves: a crowd of black-clad United fans move towards Leeds, and after a brief skirmish involving planks of wood and a wheelie bin, they have them on their toes.

United and City fans clash in Manchester city centre in March 2001. It was caught on CCTV and several people were later identified and convicted as part of Operation House.

Bucket and cups: celebrating the Treble with the trophies inside Old Trafford. We're as much fans as anyone, and whenever I hear the radio commentary of that Champions League final it brings it all back.

They said, 'No, we are leaving Joe Public out of it. We will come for you at six a.m. Be ready.'

We walk past them and go outside. Now the punchline of the story is that a kid from Lincoln was boxing on the bill and his dad has a door firm which he had brought on a coach that night – and it was the very doormen that had choked Benny and then pressed the fire alarm. Well, we bump into their coach. In seconds they were running around like headless chickens; the big sted-heads all left the other big sted-heads. And Benny went home with a smile on his face.

I had my fortieth birthday party and had 700 lads there. Some of the straight members were scared to bring their wives. I had it at Old Trafford and got a 4 a.m. licence. United have got on to who is having the fortieth so they have said, 'We can't not let him have it because he has paid a deposit but we are only having it until eleven p.m.' So we have to decide what clubs we will be able to get into and we decide on the Tapas Tapas bar. My birthday is August 10, and the next day is the Charity Shield, so we were going to have the party on the Saturday and jump on coaches to go down to the Charity Shield against Newcastle. We book Tapas Tapas.

On the night the police have riot vans parked outside Old Trafford and they're taking people's pictures. We had to walk a gauntlet of coppers, more police vans than you have ever seen. We have a line of limos to take us to the door, so when it comes to 11 p.m. the limo drivers have been dragged out and the limos taken off them. Each one had twenty people in it heading into town. We arrange to go to the Tapas bar at 1 a.m. We have a late bar until 4 a.m. But at 2 a.m. a high-ranking copper comes in and says, 'Shut the bar down.' As he walks in, the music from Laurel and Hardy was put on and everyone whistles it. A younger copper grabs someone to arrest him. So we say to the high-ranked copper, 'Let him go or you have got trouble.'

The copper says, 'Leave with no trouble and I will let him go.'

So we agreed. Everybody came out bladdered. Out of the 400 that should have made it to the Charity Shield about twenty-five got there.

For a laugh, twenty of us after the match one night went into town and I said we'd go to Tapas for revenge for them telling the police on my fortieth. I go in and a doorman stedhead said, 'You pay here, lads.'

I said, 'Fuckin' hell mate, either you are very brave or you are stupid. There's twenty of us and I know the owner.'

'The owner is not here tonight. I'm here. You pay there.'

I bitch-slapped him and he went down. I said, 'Fucking hell, what would have happened if I'd punched you? Go home and learn your job.'

We go upstairs to the bar. Once again a copper came in, I thought, *the cunt has got the police*. I said, 'Let's all walk out together, the one copper on his own is not going to arrest anyone.'

There was a big black doorman there now who I half knew. As we went out, he said, 'See you Paul.'

I said, 'What do you mean, see you Paul, like you are a friend of mine? You closed this club for my fortieth and you have called the police now. Let's you and me do it the old-fashioned way.'

'Paul, you don't understand.'

'I understand.' I walked off in a huff.

One of my mates caught up and explained to me that the copper was a kissogram. I had to go back and say sorry and thanks for not taking me up on my challenge.

People started to get terrified of us because we were older and we were gangsters. The vans with all the Robocops in their riot gear would drive past us and they'd shout, 'Wing, you prick.'

'Doyle, you prick.'

The Manchester police had had enough of us. We'd go to

places like London and the police would approach our twenty and say, 'You are all under arrest. We are going to take you to a local pub, you are going to stay there until two thirty, then we will take you to the ground. You will watch the match and then you are going home.' We had to sneak into London.

We were in a pub in town one night and we know we now have a big problem with the police. They are out to get us. They turn up at the pub and come in through the main doors, so we start to leave through the fire exit. About nine of us get out. We walk past their riot vans, which they have left unattended. One of the lads thought it would be a laugh to stab the tyres, so he does. We then go to get in our cars 200 yards away.

We hear a shout, 'Wing, you fat bastard, we are going to get you,' and all these Robocops are running down the street towards us. They surround the car Wing was standing next to and smash it up.

It wasn't our car.

Chapter Eight

SLASHED

MANCHESTER UNITED'S HISTORIC rivalry with Liverpool, both on and off the pitch, appeared by the early Nineties to have cooled from its dangerously hostile levels of the previous decade. The dreadful and deeply sobering effects of the Heysel and Hillsborough Disasters had cooled the activities of Liverpool's hooligan element. It also, for a while, eradicated the inflammatory 'Munich' chants directed at United's crowd. At the same time, many of the original lads on both sides, now older and wiser than in their reckless youth, were devoting their energies to money-making activities of various kinds, legal and illegal, and sometimes even found it mutually beneficial to work together or at least tolerate each other. Finally, Liverpool's relative decline as a team meant other sides, especially Leeds United and then Arsenal, overtook the Merseysiders as the Mancunians' main 'enemy'. The horrific slashings of a decade before were in the past, and ordinary supporters of both teams could for the first time in decades travel to their rivals' ground without fear.

Old habits and enmities died hard, however.

* * *

TONY: We managed to get tickets for the Main Stand at Anfield off the touts. We were on the second tier in the top left hand corner near our own fans in the Anfield Road End. When we got outside the ground we all sneaked around there. I think we went on coaches. We were in the ground and no copper knew we were there. There must have been fifty of us, and a lot wore dark clothing without thinking about it. We must have looked a bit sinister.

Just before half-time, everyone went round the back where you get the beer. A few Scousers saw us moving and soon came down. There is only a small passageway there and suddenly lads have gone into them. Bread trays, you name it, they are all being slung. We go halfway along the corridor and they are running back up the exit stairs to get out of our way. We fucked them off, then went back to where we had started.

At half-time we are still there and now there are a couple of coppers. For some reason they didn't get major reinforcements. Second half, we all sat down waiting for a goal so we can all jump up and probably spark it off again. It didn't happen. At the end of the game there was no attempt to keep us in. We go to the top of the stairs, head down, and outside is just packed. We get to the exit and a big gap opens and we face the usual shouting and bawling, 'Kill them!' We pile out together as a group and get stuck into them. There's a big brawl, the gap gets bigger and it's a good fight but we have backed them off. Police come round and a couple of lads get nicked because they have gone too far from the main mob.

Then we walk around to the Annie Road End, with some of the Scousers shouting, 'Hey, there's kids here,' and all that, trying to make out we are cunts. We weren't threatening any kids or straight members, as they well knew. Then the main United crowd came out and home we went.

We have been in the Main Stand, the Kemlyn Road and the

Kop. How many firms do that? That's what it's all about. Even with all-ticket games, we adapted and were game enough to go for it. The tickets were given to the right people. These were all the lads who knew the score. You wouldn't want one of those tickets unless you were ready for whatever came your way. You stand by your pals and fall with them.

When they came to Old Trafford, though, this was a snidey firm. They came in cars, thirty or forty of them, which was all they could muster. They met well beforehand and drove in down the M602 through Salford and came on to the main dual carriageway. One of the lads had followed them, picked them up on Burtonwood Service Station and followed in his car, so people knew they we're coming but at that time our lot were still scattered all over the place. People were told to meet up on the Salford side but had not yet got together as a firm.

A few of the lads were walking up and saw the Scousers getting out of their cars. They had bats, blades, the lot. Timo has gone straight into them with a couple of other lads but they have not stood a chance because there's not enough of them; they got there too early. Six or seven of them are on Timo and this scumbag has double-bladed him across the face. Then they have actually backed off. Timo is cut bad, really bad, right down his cheek and loads of police arrive.

From that moment, it was 'Get the Scousers.' That night a lot of Scousers suffered bad before the game. On occasion the police had let them out at the end of the game because their firm had stopped coming to look for a fight, but that night they kept them in because of what had gone on.

STEVE BARNES: There was no great mob at that game. The Liverpool lot had come off the M602 and were driving up Trafford Road and a couple got out of cars and were baiting

United fans. Timo has gone over and this guy pulled out a Stanley knife and cut him across his throat.

After the game, someone had identified the car they'd got out of and the United lot met at Pier 6 at the back of the Copthorne Hotel. They had found the car in the car park and all the heavies were there and there was a massive police presence and one of the United heads was trying to appeal to us to let them have a go at them.

'Are you aware of what has happened to Timo?' he said.

'We can't let you attack them,' we said. 'It would be a serious assault.'

They could have done anything to them.

A couple of the older Manc lot stood and watched the car with this lad in drive away. One of these guys rolled down his window and bragged about it and a United lad I knew said something like, 'We'll bide our time, even if we have to come to Liverpool to get you.' That's when I realise this particular United lad was more than a football hooligan.

Obviously there was a lot of tension when they played the following season at Anfield. United often met in the cellar bar at the Adelphi Hotel. There were possibly 200-plus and a group of Liverpool walked out from the pub opposite and walked past them and one guy said, 'I'm the guy that cut Timo from ear to ear.' He got showered with beer. In a short space of time they'd found out who this guy was anyway.

TONY: Next time we played them away, we met at dinnertime, a group of us, and it is a night game. We get into Liverpool at 2 p.m., have a drink, get where we want to be then move on to the Adelphi and plot up there. Eventually the police are there and the Scousers have grouped up, all phoning each other, and they come marching past us, with the cunt who striped Timo, biggest idiot in the world, jumping up and down shouting, 'I've done Timo and you're all getting it next.' Now we have all clocked his boat race. But this kid is just a loonball. There's no heroics there, Stanley knives and all that.

But the consequence of that was that two of his pals had been nicked and were appearing at Salford Magistrates Court. When in Salford, you are fucked. It's the law of the jungle. They have made their appearance and are on their way home and get in a car and they are now victims of the same tool. So they are saying this is for Timo. The Scousers weren't happy but that is what you get. I don't know who the two kids in the car were but they know why they got it: because Timo was slashed for no need. They only have their own pal to blame. That is not football hooliganism, that is just downright nasty and evil.

So he passes the Adelphi with his firm, so we know they are out tonight. The game goes on and there are lots of us there. We are kept in a little, but when we get out we go left. These vermin are in a side street down the road and some of the straight members go left and walk down there to go to their cars or whatever. We are walking down there, no Scouse coppers, just the two Manchester spotters. Who comes round the corner but the Scousers, five-handed with the rest behind them. Suddenly they have stopped. They have no chance because we are all on the road and pavement and all in black. These kids shit it, turn and are off. Suddenly we are in the side streets chasing them. You could see them in passageways screaming and running and pulling each other back. There was no way they wanted to get caught in those side streets, but they would have done it to straight members.

The next thing the slasher does, Liverpool are coming to Old Trafford and we want him and his pals to turn up. We had people all over the place. This time they get a double decker coach. They leave from Liverpool city centre, where everyone can see them, and make their way to Manchester. Just as the game starts the double decker turns up, monitored from start to finish by the police. When I refer to vermin, these are the type of people I mean. The police are obviously going to turn over the coach. He has got this mob together, the coach pulls up, they all get searched and what is on there? Stanley knives, bats, everything. The police put them back on the coach and sent them home. How none of them got nicked I'll never know.

They won't have it without the weapons. They have to inflict brutality on you. What a bunch of shithouses. They left the Adelphi on a double-decker coach, so what was the intention? They can't handle the pressure.

JB: We played Everton and I went with a good forty or fifty, all our heads. I didn't go into the match but went drinking in a pub near Goodison Park. I had this suicide streak in me. I watched the game in this pub and sussed out that they were mainly Liverpool fans in there, so when United scored I jumped up and celebrated. My mate thought we were going to get killed.

At the final whistle we left to wait at United's end. I was sitting with Willy, who has been shitting himself all afternoon. Then I heard this voice.

'You fucking Munich bastards.'

There are two lads and one launches into me. I get put down, a couple of kicks, and United's hooligan copper comes running forward and grabs me and arrests me. I'm going mad, saying, 'I've just been attacked,' but I get handcuffed and put in the back of a van.

I'm thrown in the wire cage with my handcuffs. This van follows United's firm and I can see running battles. It was great; I had a ringside seat. The van stops and the door slides open and a body is thrown in and gets kicked to fuck by the police. He's a Scouser. Then another skirmish and the back doors open and another bloke is pushed in next to me.

'Joe, how are you?' he says. It's Andy Nicholls. 'Fucking hell,' he says, 'your lads have turned out well today. How come you've turned up?'

'We just fancied it today.'

About thirty were arrested but released later without charge. The desk copper released us at the same time and said, 'You United fans are going to get kicked to fuck now.' There was only four United. But Andy Nicholls said, 'None of you are going to be touched.' And we weren't.

I later had to go back to Liverpool Magistrates Court and got a tip-off that Liverpool were going to be waiting for me outside court and were going to slash me, as part of a tit-for-tat for what happened to their lads at Salford Magistrates. It didn't happen, but that shows you how nasty things had become again.

Chapter Nine

THE NIGHT OF THE BALACLAVAS

MANCHESTER UNITED'S HOOLIGANS will often rate Tottenham as their most consistently active rivals from London, but they seem to reserve a particular dislike for West Ham. It may date back to 1967, when the Red Army took over Upton Park, the first major terrace success of a northern mob in the capital. In 1975, the East Enders responded with mass assaults on visiting United fans that made headlines in all of the following day's papers. From then on, the 'chaps' of both sides have been at loggerheads, rarely giving each other credit, in public at least.

West Ham's hooligan heyday stretched for roughly a dozen years, from the mid-Seventies to the police operation of the late Eighties. In that period, they were undoubtedly one of the two or three hardest soccer gangs in the country, some (though not Man United) would say *the* hardest. But by the mid-Nineties, many of their older faces, including some of the hardcore ICF, were no longer active at Upton Park, preferring to concentrate on legitimate or illegitimate business enterprises. Yet their reputation lingered, and it was still one of the most daunting grounds in the country to visit. United's boys knew that any trip there had the potential to turn to disaster.

Yet the events of what would become known as the Night of the Balaclavas, on Wednesday, 11 March 1998, actually began in another city many miles away.

TONY: Sheffield was one of the many places we would stop off at as we criss-crossed the country, as both Wednesday and Sheffield United know to their cost. Some of them have been funny times. On this particular day, Sheff United were playing QPR. We stopped off in the city on the way back from some game and were in a boozer on the edge of town, near the bus station. We were relaxing in the bar, playing pool or lounging about, when a couple of lads came up to the pool table.

One said, 'Are you QPR? Do you want it?'

The reply came back, 'We're Man United, fuck off, we've not finished our game of pool.'

The lad turned and quickly tried to leave but was even more quickly twatted on the head with a pool cue by our lovable rogue Eddie Beef, who felt obliged to twat him because he had been put off his game. Chaos briefly ensued, with these lads scrambling out.

I went for a stroll outside to see if they and others would come back. Sure enough, around the corner came about forty Sheff United, geeing themselves up for the attack. I moved to one side but was sure I was going to be the first to cop it. Yet for some reason they charged past me to the pub, which was now emptying. A fight started on the door, with a few heads on both sides getting punched.

I ran up behind the Sheffield mob, grabbed a lad in a headlock, bent him over and ran him head-first into a wall. He didn't know where he was, and when I released him he staggered briefly before collapsing. I then joined the fray, just as the first police officers were arriving at the scene. It was quickly all over, with everyone now complaining that they'd done nothing wrong and the police shrugging their shoulders and asking us to leave, which we did and went to the station to catch our train.

On another occasion we were playing at Barnsley, which I would like to say is a shithole with some right ugly cunts who try it on. But this day we weren't interested in them; we had already planned to leave early and go to Sheffield, the reason being that Liverpool were playing at Nottingham Forest and would be coming through the station on their way back.

Our game was not even over and there were 300 of us on the train to Sheffield. On arrival at Meadowhall, we were sure the police would be waiting, but nothing, so off we marched into the city and then to the station as quickly as possible. Everyone was soon roaming the platforms, on the hunt. After ten minutes the scream goes up and a small group of Scousers are legging it over the bridge to the far platform, where we can now see another group of Scousers. Everyone starts charging about trying to get to them but the few police on duty at the station try to hold the stairway. All we want is the Scousers, who are now a few platforms away. People are getting carried away, desperate to be first to reach them.

The police lead them to the top end of the platform and out of sight, and people are lobbing things in their direction. In desperation, some of the lads jump off the platforms, onto the tracks and across and up onto the Scousers' platform, but I'm not going on any tracks – I'd done it once before at Lime Street Station and that was enough.

Eventually, police dogs clear the platforms and we are herded together for our train without getting to grips with any Scousers, but we still had a laugh watching them run for their lives. We know it would have been the same if the roles had been reversed. It had been a good plan that only just failed – unlike the plan we had at West Ham.

This came about not because we were thinking about it but because we were back in Sheffield after playing Wednesday on a Saturday afternoon, relaxing in the pub before setting off home. Nothing of note happened that day and we were not interested in anything – until our football intelligence officer walked in with some Sheffield cops and started showing off in front of them. They were gloating that they had known where we'd be and that they all knew what we were up to. In fact we were up to nothing and not even hiding, but they were so pleased with themselves they even declared they would find us at West Ham on the following Wednesday night.

Now at the time, the West Ham match hadn't even entered our heads – with it being a Wednesday night we would normally make our individual ways down there by cars, train or whatever, arrive at different times and maybe meet near the ground. Anyway, the shout goes straight back to the football intelligence that they won't find us, and after a bit more banter they're off.

We soon plan what we're up to and it's only to fuck up the FI, to show them they are clueless and that when we don't want to be found, we won't be. The coach is hired, we meet up lunchtime on the Wednesday and we're off, accompanied by several cars also making their way there. Five o'clock and we're off the coach and down into the Tube, then off at the next stop. We know exactly what we're doing. We're well away and have a pub sorted out around the corner, just one street away from an overland stop for the train to Barking.

By 6:30 there's 200 of us, and we're off. The interesting thing about this plan is that one of the lads has come along with over 100 balaclavas for us to wear. It's not just a jolly boys' outing, we're going to have it with West Ham, and rightly so. We get off at Barking and go over the bridge and onto the platform for Upton Park. It's full of West Ham straight members. No-one says anything to them, as these aren't the people we're there for, and the West Ham fans know it and also say nothing.

On the Tube, then off we get and for the first time we are now on the opposite side to the market, where all the police are lined up and looking at the entrance to the Tube. We come out unnoticed in the dark, gather around and get ready for any West Ham who want it. There are plenty, spread along the road in groups. As we pass opposite the Queens we notice the FI leaning on railings, blissfully unaware of our presence.

Suddenly the shout goes up and everyone who has one puts on a bally and charges down the street. I go past the pricks on the railings and they cannot believe it, nor can the rest of the street, who are now faced with an awesome masked mob running full steam in their direction. The whole street is scattering and clambering away from us as we charge down towards the ground. The cops are left for dead at the station and it's left to the mounted police to charge at us from the ground. They throw their horses right into us like the Light Brigade at Balaclava, the road is in uproar, and any West Ham who stand to have a go or to take in the view are flattened.

As we get to the ground the police are going mental and grabbing the balaclavas off people's heads. It was a tremendous sight and any West Ham who witnessed it will never forget it. The lads were mad for it but in truth it only happened because of a bet with the police in the pub at Sheffield, a bet they never put to us again.

After the game we managed to get to Plaistow and a pub, which the police do not take too kindly to. They took all our details and fucked us off to Euston, where we dispersed to our coach and cars. The word from Manchester's finest was, you done us proper and made us look cunts. Well, not only them: we made West Ham look cunts too, something we have done on a few occasions.

STEVE BARNES: It was a funny game because we knew there would be a mob travelling, yet for once we had no phone calls and couldn't contact any informants. One did come through and give us the message that they were up for it but he didn't know where they were going. One of the lads apparently bought seventy balaclavas at, I think, Rochdale market. I heard they went to drink in the pub where Jack the Hat was shot by Ronnie Kray. I also later heard that Tony O'Neill had told the lads, 'No phones,' because he did not want any to be tipped off about what was going on that day.

I was at Upton Park Tube and my Manchester colleague, Kieran, was at Plaistow. There was no sign of anything and we were getting worried, because we wondered where they were going to turn up. So with Ray Whitworth, who was then in CO11, we went back into the Underground system and into central London to see if we could find them.

In the meantime, they turned up at Plaistow, where Kieran was with his oppo. They put on their ballies coming up the steps from the Tube and ran down the street. One of them told me subsequently that Kieran's face was an absolute picture as they ran down the road and slapped a few people. The effect it had on the locals was amazing. Nobody wanted to know this mad mob in balaclavas.

After the game the police housed them in a pub and they had discarded the ballies. We did a search under the Police and Criminal Evidence Act, which says that if there's a potential for public disorder, a Chief Superintendent can issue an order to stop, search and photograph, which we did. It was all the main men, laughing that we had not found them that day.

* * *

PAUL DOYLE: At the time we had to sneak into London for big games because of the police attention. Wing has organised a coach, all meeting in Piccadilly at the Waldorf. But if there is any trouble I'm not going to be coming back on a coach and risking arrest, so I normally follow by car. Someone decides it will be funny if we all put in a quid and send down to Cheetham Hill to the sweatshops and get 100 ballies. This kid gets two binbags full and some use badges to pull the eyehole together.

So we get down there, have our drinks and put the ballies on. Walking through the Tube station was hilarious. We get there and 500 West Ham are waiting and a copper shouts, 'My God, they're here and they're even ballied up, each and every one of them.'

West Ham must have been waiting all day for us to turn up yet they never made one bit of effort to attack us and we have never seen a firm run so fast. I would have loved to have seen us from the other side coming out of that station. In the end, though, people were getting arrested for having the ballies and coppers on horses were trying to pull them off heads. We knew we could never do that again.

Next time we played them was at the start of the following season. Beckham had been sent off playing for England against Argentina in the World Cup that summer and all the West ham were saying they were going to do him in. Well, we piled into their main pub, the Boleyn Tavern, before the game and did them.

After the game, we decided to walk to West Ham train station looking for it, a good fifty or sixty of us. None of them turn out. Their hearts have been broken, they have been done at the pub and they don't want to know Man United any more. Then two big lumps with the Cockney bounce, proper big stocky guys, walk towards us. I'm at the back, they walk through and bosh, I have hit one. He has not gone down but starts fighting with me.

Then I hear, 'It's Doyley, leave it, man to man.' I was ill. I had to go into another gear to finish the prick off. If I had known it was man to man I wouldn't have hit the prick in the first place.

TONY: Another match that stands out is our first visit to Upton Park after the 1998 World Cup, in which David Beckham was sent off in the crucial game. Boy did they hype this match up as anti-Beckham, so the East End and its hoolies are out. Well, so are we, and the train was full of familiar faces.

We arrived and caught the Tube to West Ham, got off and went straight into the Queens, which had just opened. So here we are, right on their plot, thinking it won't be long, maybe a few minutes, before they start to run up.

Half an hour later there is no sign of them coming to attack us so off we go out into the street. There's no point going towards the ground, as we'd only be herded into a holding area, so we make our way back past the Tube and down the road to another pub on our right, where we all plot up and settle down to wait for the West Ham.

After a while they are mooching about and there's a handful trying to be smart who have mingled in the pub having a pint but typical Cockney mouthy cunts. One can't resist opening his gob, so he's filled in with his mates and dragged through the door. What did they expect?

While we're in this pub, One-Punch and a few others are in the Boleyn pub on the corner next to the ground and have had it off inside, with the result that they've done a few in and come away practically unscathed. We learn of this and march down towards the ground with a few coppers trying to keep us in check, but they can't. As soon as we come in view of the market, the road erupts as West Ham pile out of the pub and fill the road, along with all the others who have been hanging about. Some of them make a charge but are swiftly set upon. They back off, which sets the tone for the remainder of the walk to the ground, though we are pelted with bottles and rocks for the rest of the way. At times we went at them with punches and kicks and made sure we weren't there as mugs. At times they tried to come behind us and steam us but we knew the score and all turned and stood and fucked them off.

The whole street was alive with violence and West Ham couldn't shake us. I have been to West Ham virtually every time we've played them over thirty years and this was a typical day when United were in town – the lads turned up and put themselves on offer. Don't get me wrong, there have been occasions when we've been lucky to get out alive; it's just a pity West Ham have never acknowledged us turning up in thirty years.

I apparently upset some people in the East End with my first book, *Red Army General*, which told a few truths about our confrontations with the Hammers, but the fact is that for years we had gone to Upton Park and had it with them, yet they never mention it in their own accounts. It was like we had been written out of history; maybe it didn't suit their image. Well, we don't leave ten minutes before the game, like they've done at Old Trafford, we leave Upton Park at the end and whatever happens, happens.

Once at the ground, the police did their best to get us in but we were not finished. West Ham tried to mingle in in the confusion but not for long, as there were fights breaking out and the Cockneys were getting fucked off. We did well, under immense pressure, to keep it together. Once in the ground, we knew that although it had been a good day, it was over, as the police would lock us in and then send us on our way back to Euston.

We returned the next season and had it off again with them, though not so much on the street before the game, as we had all been a few stops down the line drinking and the police on our arrival were more numerous. The walk to the ground was met with only a few bottles thrown in our direction and a token charge towards us, which resulted in a few idiots getting nicked.

The difference this time was that at the end of the game the police let us out and tried to hold us in the passageway which led onto the road. We were quite content until the Happy Hammers streaming past started calling it on with their insults and the odd rock thrown in our direction. Everyone is the passageway starts pushing forward towards the gate to get out on to the street, with the police battling to hold us back. This goes on for a minute or two but the sheer weight of numbers eventually pushes a gap so a little group gets through, then everyone is trying to get out. The first little group gets out, then we do, and it is going off near the Queens and the market.

We get up there and coppers are running all over and it has gone up. A group of West Ham are there in between the Queens and the railings. A few punches are thrown but there are too many of us and West Ham fuck off. Eventually the police restore order. We get on the Tube and all go back near Euston but we are not going home. People are messing about going to various pubs and we settle down on Euston Road for a drink.

It is getting late, we have been there a couple of hours, couple of coppers monitoring us, van outside the pub. Next thing, this kid shouts, 'They are here, it's West Ham.' Everyone jumps up, charges out of the double doors, pushes past the coppers and there are about forty West Ham, some crossing the road and some on the other side. They give it the, 'ICF, ICF.'

They got the fright of their lives. The kids coming across the road were back-pedalling as soon as they saw us, while we charged up towards the central reservation. They screamed 'ICF' while they all ran backwards into the side street. We were screaming, 'What are you doing? You can't fight running backwards.'

Eventually the police got us all and that was it, time to go, and we were away. They were that gutted at what we had done that they had come to Euston, a long way, to restore a bit of face. The same kid who threw a bin in this instance was the one who threw the bin outside the Queens on the same day, a big cunt. We just laughed at them.

Two months later, on 4 May 1998, I was nicked again. We were playing Leeds at home last game of the season, a late afternoon kick off, and there were murders. It was a Bank Holiday weekend and the streets were full of people partying and drinking, bottles and cans. It all started before the game; they were bringing Leeds fans across on coaches. Everyone was pissed outside OT. The first Leeds fans that turned up were getting blitzed. Coaches were arriving with no windows because they had already been put in on the Salford side. Police were trying to escort them across the forecourt. At that time, they didn't put the coaches right outside the door, they put them on the Trafford Wharf side.

Once it starts, everyone wants to join in. It was like a war trying to get to them. But I had decided it was on top for me and I would just stand to the side. It was all mental drunkenness and the barmy army at it. In fact the barmies tried to keep the Leeds out of Old Trafford. Their chant was, 'You're not getting in.' The chaos had to be seen to be believed and even though police were whacking people the crowd would not move to let any Leeds through. It was reminiscent of the times I had been to Leeds and they tried to kill people getting off the coaches, so I was smiling because they were getting it back. The police couldn't arrest anyone because they were in the middle of a continual riot.

After the game, they kept Leeds in and I wandered off on my

own because there was no more to be done. I got a couple of posters for my lad and thought I would take them home. Wandering towards town, I noticed two riot vans coming up behind. I crossed the road and they drove opposite me. They came to the lights and the right-hand indicator came on. I thought, *should I run down the side street and get off?* But I was best off staying on the street because those bastards had me. They were the proper riot coppers with no insignia, NATO-style helmets, boots, sticks, and they would kill me, so I walked over the other side. The vans came back and came steaming across the road. They pulled up with the doors fully open and them screaming my name.

'You bastard, O'Neill.'

'You fucking wanker.'

I put my hands out and said, 'What is your problem?'

Next thing, I'm on the deck with a helmet being smashed into my face as though he wants to butt me and other coppers piling on top. This is still broad daylight, one hour after the game. I'm next being swung round by my coat collar, being booted and abused. My phone and posters have gone. They have lost the plot.

I was eventually picked up. 'You think you are hard, you and so-and-so.' Et cetera. I was in a bit of pain and was trying to protect my leg because I was playing in goal in a cup final the next week. They were giving me dead legs but it was going to be my one and only cup final appearance. A couple of straight members walking past start telling them to calm down. Suddenly these straight members were chased over the hill by these mad coppers with their bats out.

I was in the back of the van and the copper says, 'Right Tony, you know the score, play the game and you will be out.' They nicked me, took me to Bootle Street, told me to keep my mouth shut and I would be out.

The sergeant is asking the thug copper my name and he is saying, 'It is a man who I know to be Antony O'Neill.' I said nothing and was put in a cell. Later I was let out and charged with a public order offence.

I told Matthew, my solicitor, that it was the same old crack, acting as though they don't know me, when all the while as far as I was concerned it was personal. I end up in Magistrates Court and as we turn a corner in the corridor they are all there and I can hear them saying:

'There's that cunt.'

'There he is, the bastard.'

Matthew and I jib into a room and get out of the way. I have never seen anyone so aggressive inside a court building as this lot.

They all stand up in court and state they didn't know me; they saw me in the street kicking out at cars and that alerted them to me. I was on my own, with no-one about, so when they asked me to stop they thought I was a mental patient. I wouldn't stop so they arrested me. That's their story.

The first copper gets up and says all this. We only ask him two questions.

'Do you know Tony O'Neill?'

'No.'

'Do you deal with football?'

'Yes.'

Same story from copper number two. We ask him the football intelligence question and if he knows me. Then copper number two says, 'Aah, I think I have seen Mr O'Neill's photo.'

Copper three denies knowing me before my arrest but is now told what the other two have said. He admits to knowing me because he doesn't know what else to say. The fourth and fifth coppers now admit to knowing me.

Number six copper comes up, a small chap with a beard, and starts giving evidence. He must have known it was on top because the others would have told him. In the meantime, a few of the lads have turned up and are sitting in the public gallery in the courtroom. Once Matthew starts questioning him he loses it and starts accusing everyone in the court of being football hooligans, shouting, 'They don't scare me, sitting in their pubs planning violence on their mobile phones.' Then he rattles off other things that were nothing to do with the case. But by then it had become apparent that he too clearly knew some of the lads sitting there, which rather scuppered the police claims that they didn't know who I was.

The magistrates returned after only five minutes and found me not guilty. We were all congratulating each other outside when my brief told me he had been worried all the way through. I asked him why and Matthew replied, 'To be truthful, Tony, I've not done a trial for two years, but I didn't want to tell you before we went in.'

You would think they'd have learned from their mistakes, but from the day Sgt Fox first set up the football intelligence unit, they have said in court that they didn't know who I was when they arrested me, even when evidence suggests they do know me. When I think of some of the stunts they have pulled on me, I sometimes wonder why I didn't give it all up years ago.

Chapter Ten

HOOLIGANS ABROAD

WHILE THE MANCHESTER football intelligence team did their best to prevent violence at home, when United travelled abroad – as they now did with increasing frequency – the officers had no powers of arrest and relied on foreign police forces to act on their intelligence. The notion of football intelligence was novel, if not actually unheard of, in most countries of the world, and the Manchester bobbies found a mixed quality of response on their working trips to Europe.

Fans of English teams had long run riot on the Continent, United included. By the Nineties, with other nations such as Italy, Germany, Holland and Belgium having developed their own serious hooligan problems, the issue of policing volatile international matches was high on the agenda. Co-operation between the different forces was a hit-and-miss affair.

STEVE BARNES: The police forces of the Latin countries generally didn't have a clue. Nor did the former Eastern Bloc countries. I remember going to Kosici in the Slovak Republic and they were very much a reactionary force; they'd wait for something to happen and then move in with sticks. Let's put it

141

this way, we didn't learn anything new from them in terms of approaches to combating hooliganism.

I went to Turin with United three years on the run. The first time, there was only about seventy in the main group. Outside the ground was a café bar and this seventy were sitting there having a drink. We were there with Italian police and told them who to watch. Unfortunately we were only equipped with mobile phones with poor signals, no walkie-talkies, so our only communication with control was through the police officer who was with us.

United's mob weren't moving, then suddenly a call comes over the radio: 'Emergency, officers required.' Trouble somewhere. So the two policemen with us and all the others immediately jumped in a car and zoomed off, leaving Kieran and me on our own.

Our lot immediately realised, game on. They looked over and grinned, put down their pints and all walked towards the Juve end, had a scrap, then came back to the bar. By the time the Italian cops arrived back they were all sitting there sipping beer as though nothing had happened. And there wasn't a thing we could do about it.

TONY: Going abroad is usually just a pleasure for the lads but there are certain places where you can take your life in your hands, where the locals are crazy and the police even worse. In 1991, while waiting for Operation Mars to come to trial, we played in Moscow. This wasn't a hooligan trip; this was me and my pal going on Aeroflot to Russia to watch United. There were maybe about 600 United at the game.

We met the players in Red Square the day before, and also visited the ground, playing football on the pitch. I'd had half an acid and was tripping. We end up coming out of the ground, me and my mate Mario, Simmo and a couple of others. We get to this corner and me and Mario are out of it and a gang of Russians appears. One of our group has had a piss in an entry and they start shouting about it. Meanwhile I'm on acid, the sun is shining and I'm doing circles in the street.

This gangs comes over. One has a wine bottle smashed in half and they have no shirts on. They are nutters. This was definitely not in the plan; it was not the sight-seeing trip I had envisaged. What am I going to do? They say they want my shoes. Mario is stood in the middle of the street, oblivious. I make a move towards him as the bottle is just about to be shoved in his head and there is an old woman with a big bag and she jumps in front of him screaming and they didn't do it. So I drag him across the street. There was about eight of us. We speak no Russian, there are no taxis and it is getting dark.

We walk along the street and there are no road signs or lights, it is just dim, dull blocks of flats. We cross the road at a roundabout and go in a doorway. It's a bar on an estate. We get this table in a corner. I look round and there are broken noses, thick moustaches, the lot – the local gangsters. I'm in the middle of Moscow on some council estate. I go to the bar to order some food and drink and all I can see is a picture of a chicken. Anyway the bloke behind the bar speaks decent English, so I order eight chicken and chips.

Little did we know there was no such thing as chicken on the menu in Russia in that period. Instead this pigeon, or sparrow, lands on our plates. This sets us all off laughing. The bar boss comes over to me – it's always me – and says, 'You are taking the piss.'

'What do you mean?'

He was basically saying they were going to do us in. I had to explain to him that back in England we were on the dole and had no money but fortunately we are not poor over here and we were just laughing at our good fortune. In other words, a load of lies. It worked and he calmed down.

We don't want to go out on the street, so they get us these cars, these little Trabants. Two pull up outside the bar and we run out and dive into them with our legs sticking out the doors and they drive us back to our hotel near Red Square. We promise him $10 but then rush up the steps into the hotel without paying. He couldn't come and get his money because the taxi rank at the hotel door is run by the mafia. We are in the hotel and end up drinking more. Champagne was $3 and even at that price we were getting ripped off but we were happy.

Next night we are in the game and it is dismal. The only spectacular thing to happen was that we finally found a McDonalds – which a few weeks later got a grenade thrown in it. We lose and are knocked out of the Cup Winners Cup. The game ends and there is a lot of abuse from the sides but that doesn't worry us. We are kept in, while the abuse keeps coming from out of the darkness outside. They finally take us round the pitch, behind one goal and through these double gates.

The Russian fans are fighting like mad against soldiers with long sticks guarding the coaches. We aren't going to the coaches but we can't move because the Russians aren't moving. We have to go left because we know there's a couple of people on a coach going back to the centre. Mario and I delay too long and end up with the Russians. I have got a big overcoat on and I keep my head down. We even join in their chants, just mumbling the words. Believe me, when your life is in danger you can mingle in.

We have to get on the coach back to the hotel, but it is surrounded again. Then came one of the funniest things I have ever seen. The door on the coach, a crammed fifty-seater, is not opening. It's already got 125 people on it, terrified. The coach is getting ready to go and if it does, Mario and I are dead. It starts to pull away.

In his desperation and fear, Mario runs out of the crowd of

Russians and jumps with arms wide onto the front windscreen of the coach, his feet on the bumper and his face pressed against the glass, virtually staring into the eyes of the startled driver. No thought for me, every man for himself. The Russians are also startled and can't figure out if it's one of their own on a suicide mission or some crazy Englishman.

A girl on the coach recognises him and shouts, 'Open the door, it's Mario.'

He climbs round to the front and squeezes in. The Russians by this time are all howling with laughter and so they don't make a move.

Mario is now yelling, 'Leave the door open, Tony is out there.'

Now it's my turn to dive out of the crowd and climb on.

I swore after that I would never go to Moscow again. The thought was in my head that I could have been done in and killed for the sake of someone wanting my clothes, and no-one would give a toss. It's still bad now but back then it was lawless.

In the autumn of 1997, Manchester United played Dutch giants Feyenoord in the European Champions League. The Dutch, along with the Germans, had long been considered England's major rival in the international hooligan scene, and in some quarters the match was seen as a clash between two of the toughest and most battle-hardened hooligan gangs in Europe.

TONY: Only once in modern times, at Rotterdam, did we seriously look for trouble abroad. We played them at home and they didn't bring a big mob; everyone was waiting but there was no mob, just a few punches in the ground. We all knew the score, so it was off to Amsterdam and we knew we were up against it, especially as we were given only a small ticket allocation. We were all there for a couple of days and decided to get the 4 p.m. train to Rotterdam.

It was an afternoon of pure noise and drunkenness, then at 4 p.m. came this amazing sight of everyone getting up and marching together down the street to the train station without anyone having to say a word. We got on one of those double-decker trains and filled it and everyone was buzzing. I could see Manchester Old Bill running around on the train station and knew that outside would be 200 Dutch police with horses, water cannons, rottweilers, the lot.

I lead the mob outside and go through the exit doors at the front of the station. All these coppers are lined up to make us go right. But there were no coppers to the left, so I turned left and as everyone piled out they followed me. Incredibly, the police just stood there and watched. I didn't know where I was going but suddenly 400 of us were across the car park at a fast trot before the police got it together. Still they stood and watched. The only people to follow us were Manchester football intelligence, who had no powers or authority abroad.

We broke into a run. One or two kids at the front were saying where Feyenoord's mob would be. The plan was to get them because of reports of United fans being beaten up during the day. They were all said to be in a main square. I didn't know where the square was, but there was a Dutch kid there who showed us. Straight ahead, turn left, turn right and it was there. One of the Manchester FI is right next to me screaming into the phone, 'They know where they are!' If we had not been on friendly terms he would have been smashed in the head.

We run around this corner and there are all these bars with the Dutch outside and we have come from nowhere and steamed into them. We clear the square. Unbeknown to us, this square is also where all the TV crews are stationed because there is some sort of event going on there. So as we blitz all these bars it is all being filmed. Chairs and tables are going. It is amazing that the police never came. Bars and people have been smashed up. When it is virtually over, because there is nothing left to do, a few riot police come running around the corner. I change my top and no-one gets arrested.

So now we march down some shopping area, a business district and again there are no police with us. I said, 'What we need to do before there is a comeback from Feyenoord is find somewhere, get together and get ready for it.' We are expecting reprisals. Go down a couple of streets and there is a load more bars. After about twenty minutes the only people who turn up are the odd copper stood on corners. Quite friendly, no hassle, no big police presence yet we have got several hundred United fans packed in these bars and in the street but it is like a Sunday afternoon picnic. It was as though the police were quite happy for it to go on and for us to teach Feyenoord a lesson.

Eventually they brought the buses for us, double-deckers. They put us on them, no evil treatment, no aggression. They were all happy. We get taken to a square where the straight-member coaches are parked. We try to get away from there but mounted police drive us back and we are driven to the ground.

As we get there it is dark, all massive car parks. Stones hit the windows but when we look out we can't see anything clearly. We know people are there but we can only see figures and shadows running in the dark. We come to a junction and stop at traffic lights. The first double-decker goes round but we are stuck at the lights and we can see Feyenoord in the car park. We can see where the first coach is going to pull up outside the away end and we see all these bodies appear from the car park going towards it. The door opens and it is going off. Some are throwing planks of wood at the bus. We go mad and fight to get off to help our lot. This went on for two minutes as the police fought us back, while we can see it going off around the first bus.

But Feyenoord don't properly continue their attack. One of the well-known Cockney lads is off the bus with a few more and then others follow and they make a stand and we can see punches being thrown. Eventually our bus gets going and parks up. Feyenoord are still in the car park – they should have come up the banking and swarmed the place but they didn't. We are running around now because we want a bit.

Wing, in his wisdom, decides he's going on a march around the ground. He gets a few together, goes over the bridge and makes the other end, which is a massive open space near a railway station. There's about seventy in this firm and suddenly it's right on top. There's coshes being pulled out, the first few punches go in and it looks bad for Wing's mob. The only thing that saved them was that the police came rushing in and quelled it. Another minute and they would have been butchered. It did result in one of the lads getting arrested and jailed.

In the ground, Feyenoord were all trying to kick down the fence between us. There's a big door in the middle of this fence, which goes from the front of the pitch to the back, and there were no police there. The kicking is booming and all these guys are singing, 'Rotterdam, hooligans, Rotterdam, hooligans.' I touch this handle and the gate opens in my hand. It opens towards me, so I open it and that is it. They come rushing to the doors and we start punching them and holding them off. Everyone is grappling with each other and in the end I shut it until there are more of us. Then I open it again.

I must have opened this about seven times, and each time there was a fight. I'm trying to pull people in to our side and it's getting ridiculous. This was in full view and went on for ten minutes. But if someone went through, you had to get them out. I shut the door at one point and they start ripping up some wall or floor and there are half-bricks coming through on to our side.

I get a full brick. You can't see through this fence but you know there are loads of them behind. For the last time I'm getting ready to open the door. I pull it open and smash the brick full in someone's face. I had to shut the door for good in the end and by then the riot police had turned up and we were shattered anyway.

Then we had the usual banter because they were on both sides of us and they did not want to watch the match. We felt we were right up against it after the game, but they kept us in. We went there and took it to them. It was two armies going at it and was the first time it had happened for a long time.

JB: A good 400 lads piled out of the station and this Dutch kid met us. 'I take you to their boys. I take you right there.'

We walked up and there was a continental-style bar with big full-length windows and awnings and a massive Feyenoord flag in the window. Me and Tony and this big Cockney just ran up, picked up a chair and smashed it through the window. There were some big cunts in there, but everyone attacked the bar – and that was our arrival in Rotterdam.

STEVE BARNES: We knew when the draw was made the ones that attracted them. Feyenoord was one and Dortmund was another problem game, a lot of fighting. Those two were musts for the lads, and on big foreign games the gangster element would also turn out.

Feyenoord was pure mob, 3–400 lads all in Amsterdam beforehand. Our top informant had told us the plan from the beginning and we relayed it to the intelligence in Holland. We knew exactly what was coming, but I don't think Feyenoord's boys did, otherwise they would have been ready.

On the train to Rotterdam, I was in the drivers' compartment, while Kieran went by car. The train driver locked the door and I told him not to open it under any circumstances. There were no uniforms aboard, just me and my Dutch opposite number. We kept ringing the intelligence cell on the journey, saying, 'We are at such and such a station, estimated time of arrival twenty minutes, etc.'

When we arrived at the station, Kieran was already there with his opposite number. The United mob walked through about fifty riot vans and kept on going and the police didn't move a muscle. Kieran was waiting at the front, I came through at the back, and when we met we just looked at each other as if to say, 'Why aren't the police stopping them?'

We later found that in the Dutch police chain of command, an intelligence officer can't tell the riot police what to do. He has to radio in to his commander, who then has to inform the riot police commander, who then has to decide how to deploy his men and pass the message down to them. Because there was no-one there with the authority to tell them to follow the United mob, the riot police stayed where they were. Their orders were to be at the station, and that's where they were staying until they were told otherwise. So the United lads walked right past them and into the town centre, with only Kieran and I and our two Dutch counterparts. They knew we were with them but they didn't care – what were we going to do?

The rumour was that they were met by two Arnhem fans who knew where Feyenoord would be. Once we got to the square, it went off like I'd never seen. It was incredible. Kieran and I stood there in a shop doorway and watched windows go in and people getting slapped. There was nothing we could do, so we just stood ringside and watched it all. There was loads of wrought iron furniture and pot plants and I think there were two bars next to each other and they got trashed. They were fighting for twenty minutes, no kidding. The Dutch fought back but they were hammered, well and truly, and I don't think any United got injured. We didn't have a camera but there must have been someone with a camera because I'm sure there is a photo of O'Neill throwing something through a window.

The riot police then just corralled them in and marched them to a pub. Kieran and I went along to supervise and they were ecstatic. They were saying to us, 'What a well-planned operation that was. Where were you guys? What were you doing?'

We said, 'Don't you mean, what were the Dutch police doing? We were there.'

The Dutch cops told us Feyenoord were the bullies of the Dutch league, so they were quite happy to see them get a pasting.

There was then fighting outside the stadium, mass fighting all over the forecourt. It was just bedlam. There didn't seem to be any police operation at all at the ground.

TONY: In April 2002, we played Bayer Leverkusen in the Champions League semi-final. The lads were milling around their ground and no-one was expecting trouble when suddenly they were there; they turned up in white minibuses and were big steroid-heads in black bomber jackets, boots, gloves. We later found out they weren't Leverkusen fans but had travelled several hundred miles from another German city to have it with the English. They'd assumed that we would be looking for trouble but they couldn't have been further from the truth. We rarely look for trouble abroad, if we have any it has usually come to us.

Anyway, this lot really want it. We go straight into them but they give as good as they get. They were game kids and all seemed to be doormen types, weightlifters, thick necks. But the lads soon found they had rules as well. When one of the lads got put down, they stopped and didn't follow through on him. But once one of them went down he got several boots to the head because we don't want the big lump to get back up.

In the end the Germans stopped and said, 'Well done.' Then a couple of them came over and said, 'Can we join up with you?' They wanted to go to some train station after the game because they were saying Cologne would be waiting there for United to come back and they wanted to have a go at them. We told them to fuck off.

The next time we went there, in September the same year, everyone was heading back to Cologne and thanks to them we knew what to expect, unlike the Scousers who had once been smashed all over there. I couldn't go back to Cologne because I had to jump on a plane to get back to the UK for a court hearing the next morning. But while I was at the airport, United came out of the train station and Germans attacked from the side streets, throwing. Our lot were braced for it and blitzed them all over the streets. The Germans were there to take liberties but the lads did a good job and saved a lot of straight members from getting a hiding.

When we played Dortmund in the semi-final in 1997 it was the same type of people. They were hanging around the railway station early in the morning and you could see a couple of them and you knew it was going to go off in the city centre. While we were in a couple of bars, it has gone off and the Germans have attacked some United fans, who weren't all mugs. They really had a set-to and were lucky to hold their ground.

There were scuffles at the ground with them as well, and this time the lads blitzed them across the lawn of a nearby hotel. When they got on the pavement outside the ground the German police surrounded them, brought the vans, threw them in and then took them to a hangar. They let them out after the game. There were a few scuffles after because the Germans were right up for it, but no mass brawl. One of the German swag sellers ended up in a headlock bent over a bin. But he screamed that loud there was a truncheon laid across my back and I had to let him go.

When it is a hard ticket to get for a game, the foreign touts tend to cop it. When we played a semi-final at Monaco, we enticed a tout into a side street and he literally had the back pockets ripped off his jeans, had his throat nearly torn out to stop him screaming and was picked up bodily and thrown through the air. Touts were just having their tickets grabbed off them. If you can't get in you revert to the old way of knocking the door in. We did the door when we went to Middlesbrough last game of the season and won the League. We got in a bit early and told people what gate was going to be flung open. The steward was bundled away, the locks came down and they were all there piling in, right on cue. You can't lock your exit doors for safety reasons.

It was unusual for foreign teams to bring a firm to Old Trafford. Anderlecht did come one year. By 1 p.m. there were about 1,000 of them stood outside here and by 3 p.m. there were 2,000. They were getting drunk and giving it the big 'un but there were no United there until about 5.30, not that the lads were likely to turn out for a European night. But by 6 p.m. about eighty have got together and are on a side street. The police try to move the Belgians on down Sir Matt Busby Way to the ground but it is taking ages, so there is like a big march to the ground. A couple of their lads have been sussed bouncing up and down in the road, unopposed, one guy with a ponytail.

The eighty go down the side street like the old days and come charging out by the ground, straight into them and right through them. Their lad with the ponytail was the first to fuck off. This eighty whack them and it goes off in the middle of the street but the police force United's mob back into the side street and they return to the pub.

So now it looks likely to go off after the game, for the first time at a European tie for ages. A nearby pub filled with United's boys while they kept the Belgians in the ground for ages. The police lined the forecourt and then they came out, about forty-five minutes after the end of the match. They were forced to go towards the coaches. All the United lads came out of the pub, down the side street and over the bridge on the other side of the road. There must have been 150 police but they let this United mob walk alongside them as they are marching to their coaches and as we go over the Salford-side bridge, smash, we go into them and are whacking them all over. We tried to charge the coaches and the horses came in.

So now we have to go to Anderlecht. We know it is going to be tough so we are all there and slowly shoot off because there is a lot of police activity. Also most of us haven't got tickets because they were in very short supply for that game. We get on the underground in little groups, plot up in a little bar then get to the ground to this bar area, and it is packed with them all. We are on a suicide mission, only about seventy of us but we are having it.

We march out of this side street into the crowd and then stop as if to all bunch up. We were just about to kick it off when we eyeball these FI officers in plain clothes, three of them. They have eyeballed us and radios are going and coppers are running with their shields from everywhere. They blocked us in and led us away and I was glad, because we would have been killed; there were loads of them in that square area. In the end there was no trouble at all then.

Chapter Eleven

THE MEN IN BLACK

BY THE END of the decade, United's mob had forged a reputation second to none in the hooligan world. They were organised, confident, cohesive and ruthless. One thing they didn't have, however, was a name to go with that reputation. They had always shunned the kind of gang names adopted by others, regarding them as childish. Apart from 'Red Army', the only name that had ever really stuck around was ICJ, the Inter City Jibbers, whose motto was 'To Pay is to Fail'. To most, the hooligan element were simply 'the main boys'. But with their persistent, indeed growing, activity, it was perhaps inevitable that someone would attach a label to them – and when they did, it was memorably apt.

TONY: The name Men In Black came after another busy day at West Ham. The funny thing about that day was that on our way down on the train, the conversation was all about how it was time we had to slow down the violence, as over the past few years we had been causing mayhem and the police were getting sick of us. We knew we were going to hit the buffers.

For the past ten years we had been travelling in large numbers away from home, and as far as I am concerned were the only Premiership mob to be doing so on a weekly basis: some for the violence, some for the protection a large mob affords them, and some for the thieving. Also half of us were 'allowed' to travel by train for nothing – the police would often put a large firm straight on the train without asking for tickets as they were only interested in containing us.

We stopped off a few stops before Upton Park, where by noon about 400 had gathered for a drink and to wait and see if West Ham arrived. But they didn't bother before the game and we saw none. We duly arrived at 2:30 and were marched to the ground. We made no effort at confrontation, as that was the general feeling. West Ham also seemed subdued so it was just the usual eyeballing and weighing each other up.

All that changed when we came out at the final whistle. The police made us file out in a narrow line, which gave some West Ham the idea that here was a chance to have a go at a few United, and they launched an attack. As soon as you hear a roar but can't see what's going on you automatically want to get there so suddenly down the passageway hundreds tried to surge past the police. Chaos now reigned, with us battling the boys in blue.

All our previous discussions before the game about our days being numbered and not winding up the police now evaporated as the surge towards violence was now on. Police were struggling to hold us back and we could see groups of West Ham egging us on, no doubt thinking we wouldn't break through.

The struggle continued for a couple of minutes, with the police using truncheons on those at the front and even bringing in horses, but the sheer weight of numbers won the day. At first a few Cockney Reds and Mancs got up the road, followed by the rest of the firm, and we were back-pedalling any West Ham in front of us until we reached the outdoor market, where a few punches were thrown and dustbins were chucked at each other, nothing vicious but to us it was a job well done. We could see in their eyes that they were ill, as we had cleared the street and they couldn't do anything about it.

We all boarded the train with no hassle, as the police were now in charge. The train must have held up to 1,000 Reds and off it went with us thinking it would go non-stop to Euston. But for some reason we stopped at Aldgate East. Well, a large number of us decided this would be a good place to get off, so we left the train with the police powerless to stop us. We soon found a boozer, which couldn't hold us all, so hundreds were hanging about outside on the road searching for another pub or two nearby, on Brick Lane.

After ninety minutes in the pub, about seventy of us at the bottom of Brick Lane began heading back when a call was received from the first pub, informing us that there were only a few left there, as everyone else had made their way back to Euston. We told them we wouldn't be long, which was just as well, as within a minute of us arriving back at the first pub, the shout of 'West Ham are here!' went up.

Most of the group who had come back were outside the pub or in the burger bars dotted along the road. I rushed out of the pub to see a mob who had obviously come out of the Tube station. They were charging towards us shouting, 'ICF!' Well we were already charging towards them. This looked like it was really going to happen, no police, nothing to stop us – this was it. As we came nearer to each other you could make out some of these were from the early skirmishes along the High Street at Upton Park, so headlong we carried on.

West Ham running at you shouting 'ICF' is old hat. It might have once terrified people but it had the opposite effect on us, largely because down the years we had come to despise all the bullshit about their legendary ICF, as if they ruled the world.

Well, their boys showed themselves up this day. Twenty yards from smashing into each other, they bottled it, turned and ran. The word really is that they crumbled, big time. We chased them across the road and the bulk of the ICF mob legged it into the Tube station, quickly followed by us. By the time we had vaulted the ticket barriers and got properly in there, they were gone, as quickly as that.

We got back out on the street and bounced about looking for any remnants of their firm, but they had gone. The only person who hadn't moved was one of our lads who was flat on the floor, having been run over by a car, but he wasn't seriously hurt. The buzz soon took him over and he was back on his feet and with us heading back to Euston with a police escort and onto the train to Manchester, as this was an all-Manchester firm.

We were buzzing even more when the inevitable phone call came through from Wing, who wanted to know what had happened. He was sat on a riverbank somewhere – having chosen to go fishing instead of to the game – but had taken a call on his mobile from some West Ham kid, which he now relayed to us. Apparently this kid had been one of those we had chased and had told Wing he couldn't believe it, as all he saw was loads of people emerge from behind trees and out of doorways and run towards them, all dressed in black. 'These facking men in black just came from everywhere,' he said, or words to that effect.

This was something we hadn't even thought about, and we all fell about laughing. For the next few days we jokingly called ourselves the Men In Black, and it became an unofficial nickname which we adopted for the crack. It even began to work for us, as you do look the part all togged up in black gear, even though it was never a planned look or image, just something that came about through the dress code and designer labels of many of the lads.

———————

No sooner had they received their new 'name' than some of their most feared members were removed from the scene. In March 1999, the *Manchester Evening News* carried a front-page story under a huge banner headline:

SWOOP ON THE UNTOUCHABLES

The biggest-ever attack on criminals in Greater Manchester swung into action today when police carried out dawn raids on more than 60 homes.

The swoops came after officers infiltrated the criminal community in the Salford area over eight months, buying drugs and stolen property from villains.

Operation Victory – the largest of its kind outside London – was set up to target 'untouchable' criminals who have tarnished the city's reputation and persistent offenders.

About 500 officers from Greater Manchester Police raided 66 addresses.

A total of 53 people were arrested – 43 men and 10 women – and are in custody at 10 police stations across the force. Those who are charged will appear before Salford magistrates tomorrow.

Police seized a sawn-off shotgun and two pistols, along with drugs including amphetamines, LSD, cannabis, ecstasy, cocaine and heroin with a street value of £250,000.

They recovered stolen property including TV sets, computers, garden equipment, a concrete mixer, musical instruments and . . . a tractor.

Chief Supt Chris Wells, head of Salford Police, said: 'This was a very successful operation aimed at the most prolific and high-volume criminals.'

The biggest fish snared in the Operation Victory net was Paul Doyle. With some of his close associates, he had been targeted by specially trained detectives – ironically from the Omega Squad, first set up to combat the hooligan gangs more than ten years earlier – in an undercover operation. The weight of evidence forced him to plead guilty to conspiracy to supply cocaine and cannabis, and at the age of forty-one he was jailed for seven years.

At about the same time, several other key members of United's football firm were jailed for involvement in a separate conspiracy to smuggle more than two tonnes of cannabis, worth £8 million. They were arrested after police and customs officers intercepted a lorry at an industrial unit in Rossendale, Lancashire. Given that some of the 'Men in Black' were believed by police to have moved many tonnes of cannabis over the previous few years, it was inevitable that some of them would finally be caught.

For men like Paul Doyle, who had spent time in institutions since childhood, jail was an occupational hazard. He devoted his energies inside to a punishing personal fitness programme of burpees and press-ups that would see him emerge, if possible, even tougher than before. Today he focuses on legitimate business activities.

PAUL DOYLE: They surrounded me in the box with armed cops and there were riot vans outside the court. I had gone well beyond local football police. It was Interpol. I was involved with mass murderers and top international criminals. They wanted to put me away for twenty years. Even at the end of my court case, the maximum sentence they could give me was seven years and they gave me seven.

When you go away, you get put on a shit wing at the beginning. Two days later, United were playing Juventus at Old Trafford in the Champions League. I knew all the servery lads and got given loads of food. This screw put me on another wing so I said, 'Do you fancy going to the match? I'll get you tickets.' I used to give them to all the screws. I made sure all the lads had a cushy time. I got them Wembley tickets, VIP treatment.

A while later, the papers ran a big story saying that a Salford Mr Big had been dishing out tickets to prison warders in return for favours and they had launched a big inquiry. Only thing was, they blamed Paul Massey [another Salford criminal] for it. Massey sent me a letter saying, 'Why do I get the blame for everything you do?'

Now I go to matches with my kids. It would be totally embarrassing at my age to be pulled up for fighting at a football match. I have moved on to bigger and better things.

STEVE BARNES: The truth is, nobody could touch them on a full turnout, not in my time. I'm not taking pride in that, it's just a fact. I never saw them come unstuck. Yet I never feared for my safety at any time with them. We never felt in any danger from the main boys and there was definitely control by the main boys of the rest, especially by Tony. They knew the score. They weren't going to take me on; they knew if they did they would never set foot inside a football ground again.

As the football intelligence unit, we didn't do undercover operations. Alan Hutchings was the match commander and felt the idea of undercover stuff was too expensive, with him doing the budget. He just wanted to keep the lid on it, especially at home, and we were happy with preventing disorder. There were some problems at Old Trafford with Leeds and Liverpool on the forecourt, but that was mainly what they called the barmies and nasty stuff being shouted about Munich and Hillsborough. There were some big turnouts and mobs of 100–150 that came, like Tottenham, who walked all the way back into town after the game, and Sunderland a few years ago, but most of the time we were on the ball with them. Away from home was a different matter.

People have tried for years to explain why hooligans do what they do. I always liken it to a young police officer who gets a call that there is a fight in a pub. He can't wait to get there, but contrary to what people may believe, he's not dashing there because he wants to do his duty and help the public; he is getting there because he wants to pile in and smash heads. It is the same mentality. It is a buzz, exciting, regardless of what academics say about people's working class backgrounds, being drink-related, and so on – it is exciting.

I knew organisation was a bonus, and they were organised whereas other groups weren't. If this group stood together, it says an awful lot. Tony was unique in that he always seemed to do things with a smile on his face, as though it was a game. Loyalty is the wrong word, but I could only do my job – which to me and my boss was stopping fights – if I had my credibility among the hooligan group. If I was to arrest them, or even if I was openly seen to be pointing out people in that group to be arrested, my credibility would be in question.

One example happened at a game at Villa Park. Tony was clearly leading the group, and this West Midlands inspector I was walking next to said, 'Who is the tall guy in the middle shouting the odds?' He was obviously going to lock him up, but everybody in the United mob heard this question and they all went quiet waiting for me to answer.

I got round it by saying, 'I don't know who he is but I'm going to find out.' I then shouted across, 'Hey gobby, keep your fucking mouth shut.' Tony came back with, 'Sorry boss.' He knew what was going on. There was no reason to arrest him then because they weren't going to fight, not with us beside them. If they had gone in for Tony it could also have meant policemen assaulted, because a lot of the lads would have reacted. I took this inspector over to one side afterwards and explained that I did of course know Tony and told him what the situation was. He understood.

But things were coming to an end for me, though I didn't know it. In December 1998, we played a league game at Tottenham. It was dark, could have been a late kick-off. There was a large mob of about 300 United. We found them early and they housed themselves in a pub on Tottenham High Road and we walked them down, escorted them into the ground, not much trouble pre-match. Post-match, they were going to walk down Seven Sisters and take on all comers. That was what we found out.

We came out of the ground onto Tottenham High Road and the Met said about seventy Spurs were out but once it goes off you can expect others to join in. United were on one side on the pavement, spilling into the road, and Spurs on the other. Every so often there would be a surge from one side to the other and they were batted back by the police after a few quick punches and kicks had been exchanged.

Then there was a big surge forward by Tottenham about twenty yards in front of me and I started running forward to get there, thinking I could prevent something from happening. I was then hit between the shoulders from behind by what I can only describe as a cannonball and was knocked flat on my face. As I lifted my head I saw that I had a horse's front legs either side of my head and I was right underneath the horse. As the horse moved off, its back leg kicked me in the head behind the left ear.

I think I was out for two or three seconds. Next thing I remember was being lifted up by Metropolitan Police officers. Some of the United boys were a bit concerned and were shouting, 'Steve, are you all right?' I had a sore head which was gradually swelling behind my ear. I carried on walking and put them on the Tube, went back to the station and the sergeant called out the police doctor, who examined me and said it was probably just bruising. He didn't think I needed an X-ray and gave me some Paracetamol. We went back to our digs in Kentish Town and had a few drinks. I went to bed and woke in the night with a roaring headache, but over the next few days the swelling went. It was a busy season and the job had to go on.

All the seasons I was involved there was lots of trouble, and the problems got bigger and bigger. The figures showed it was increasing from 1995–99. The success on the pitch and the glamorous trips they were going on swelled the numbers. The only time I saw them in trouble came the following year, 1999, at Leeds.

An operation for a game like Leeds-Man United, where you know there is massive potential for disorder, has to be intelligence-led. This one clearly wasn't. There were three of us from Manchester – me, Kieran and Ken – and we went out in the morning with two intelligence officers from Leeds. Meanwhile all of the riot police are at the police station having their breakfast.

We waited at the train station to see our lot out and Tony O'Neill led about 150 United out onto the street. We got out of the van and walked with them. Kieran and his oppo were with United, and I was with Stan, their well-known spotter, and the Leeds lot. As Leeds came out of the pub and walked down the road, United appeared and the two mobs were about thirty yards apart.

I said to Stan, 'For fuck's sake Stan, where are all the police?'

'I'll just radio in,' he replied.

It should have been World War Three. There were probably about 150 United and must have been 3–400 Leeds, with only five of us between them in riot gear. Stan whacked Tony on the legs to keep him back but I knew from their body language that the United lot weren't going to go into them. They knew there were cameras there and were standing to let Leeds come at them, so they could then plead self-defence if they were caught fighting. Stan was shouting, 'I've got CS gas, I've got CS gas.' Yet even though there were only five police there wasn't a massive scrap. The officers in between them were the ones that knew them all, and that must have been a deterrent.

Meanwhile the riot police were still in the nick. Eventually they turned up but the bottles had been thrown by then. The United lot were then housed in a pub and there were a few attempts to get to them, but by that time all the riot police were there. The United lot had walked into their city centre and shown out to Leeds and Leeds had not responded properly by their lights, so half of the task had been completed.

When they did march them to the ground, the riot police corralled them against a wall with dogs and wouldn't push the Leeds lot back. United were surrounded and massively out-numbered and were getting a hammering from a hail of bottles – the Leeds hooligans were just being allowed to throw things. So Kieran, Ken and I decided we were going to push them back. We had the full-face helmets, steel toe-capped boots, side-handled batons, and we waded in. It was fantastic. I felt like I had done a training session when I got back.

We returned to a standing ovation off the United lads. Their match commander said, 'I don't think that's quite the reaction I want from a hooligan mob towards police officers.'

I said to him, 'With all due respect sir, we were doing the job your officers are supposed to be doing.'

It was also part of the strange relationship we had with our hooligans, and things like that would work in our favour at a later date.

Around this time, I noticed the hearing was starting to go in my left ear. I put it down to the kick from the horse at Spurs. Eventually I saw a specialist and had hearing tests that showed I was seventy per cent deficient in that ear. I had an MRI scan on my head and they found what they called a growth in my inner ear. I was then told it was an acoustic neuroma, a tumour behind my left eye the size of a golfball – and it was growing. They said they would have to perform twelve hours of neurosurgery with the potential that I might die because it was such a serious operation. On the other hand, if I didn't have the op I would likely die anyway.

It wasn't a happy time. Fortunately the op was a complete success. They got the tumour out, it was benign and it hasn't recurred. They also said the tumour was not caused by trauma, so it was the luckiest horse's kick I could have had.

I carried on doing my job until October 1999, which was when I got the results of my first test. By that time my hearing could have been a danger to me and my colleagues, so they told me I was deskbound. The realisation that I had a tumour affected me psychologically and about three weeks later I went off work sick. I never returned.

I saw all the Treble season and was just getting excited about the new draw for the Champions League and the places I would be going. They kept me on full pay, I had the op in August 2000, and then eventually I left the force.

And who were the first people to send me a get-well card after the operation? The United hooligans.

TONY: The Treble season will never be forgotten. We were untouchable on and off the pitch. You couldn't do United's firm in 1999. It was impossible.

We played Arsenal at Villa Park in the FA Cup semi-final, the first game when it was 0–0. We walked down to Aston Station after having first walked up to the Arsenal end but there was no sign of their firm on the corner looking for it. So we end up all along the road, hanging about around Aston Station. We know Arsenal have to come.

Suddenly this firm of them came swaggering down the road but out of sight of where I am. They can't see everyone around the corner and down the street. The verbal goes and it is ready to kick. We knew something was going on without even being able to see it. Then comes the shout, 'Arsenal are here.'

They come round the corner with a few United having a scuffle and get the shock of their lives. They were all there in their Stone Island gear thinking they were the coolest people on the planet but they got blitzed. They ran behind a pub and up the street and it was their main mob. Their spotter, Ray Whitworth was running alongside me with his truncheon out. I said to him, 'Put the fucking bat away before you get hurt.' And Ray with his little legs was trying to keep up with me.

The Champions League final [against Bayern Munich] wasn't about violence, though the ticket spivs got smashed. At the ground and in the streets, anyone selling tickets who the lads didn't know was getting them snatched or ending up on the floor holding his nose. The lads did actually have a fight in Lloret de Mar with the Germans and smashed them around the town. Quite a few had gone there for a few days before the game but it wasn't organised, it just happened. Bayern's lads were also there in force and thought they had the town to themselves, but not a chance. Come early evening they just got mashed. As they were running round one corner they were running round the tail of the mob chasing them and getting battered again.

The final was the best thing in my life. I nearly had a heart attack. I couldn't breathe when the first goal went in and the next one, I couldn't hear my son and he was screaming on the chair next to me. My ears had popped and my lungs were coming through my throat. I couldn't hear anything and this went on from the first goal to the second. It was the best feeling ever, and if I ever hear the commentary again or see the pictures, the hairs on my neck stand on end. There is no way in the world you can beat that script. You will never get that again. I was a kid when they won it in 1968 so it didn't really mean anything. You go all your life and that is the pinnacle for a football fan. I could watch that last ten minutes every day. So any United fan who is ever depressed, just stick ten minutes of that on. Watch the video or listen to the radio commentary, which was just unbelievable.

It would have been a great way to go, but I didn't want to go. After the game I started my own company, Champion Sports Travel, to run trips to matches. I'd always run coaches on and off but now there was the opportunity of all the European games. In truth, it was probably the worst time to do it: after the Champions League final, everyone had spent up and there was a feeling that nothing could top that anyway. But with United now playing so much European football, I was still banking on there being enough trips and enough people wanting to go to make a living.

I would very quickly get labelled by the football intelligence as the travel organiser for the mob, but nothing could be further from the truth. You can't run a business like that. The only way any small business can survive is word of mouth and personal recommendation. If my trips were dodgy or dangerous, people would not go again, simple as that. I wanted people from all walks of life on my trips – solicitors, off duty police officers, magistrates, whatever – and that is what I got.

That's not to say that certain European destinations could not be hairy – sometimes very hairy. In October 1999, we played Croatia Zagreb, who were previously called Dynamo Zagreb, and I took about forty over. We were in a decent hotel in the city centre, a few English reporters in there, and met up with a few other fans, a mixed bunch, men, women, young and old. We found a bar and were watching a game on TV, relaxing. At about 8:30 p.m., I borrowed someone's phone to make a call. For a bit of privacy and quiet, I walked over to another café opposite and sat on one of the chairs outside to make this call.

Out of the dark appeared a right firm of evil-looking bastards. They looked like squaddies, all with skinheads, bomber jackets and boots and that nasty, right-wing look. They surrounded the bar where these straight member United fans were watching football. I was sitting behind them, watching, and they hadn't noticed me. Well, believe me, I hunkered down over on that phone. I'm thinking, *fucking hell, what is this?* Next thing, they just attacked the United fans. They flung chairs and tables at them and United outside had to rush into the bar and force the doors shut, with all these psychos screaming, shouting and hurling furniture at them while trying to break in.

All the time I'm sat opposite. I couldn't lift my head because I still had a black eye from a fortnight earlier, when we had played Marseille and a steward had twatted me. If these paramilitary loons clocked my black eye they'd immediately suss I was a boy and that would be curtains for me. Not for the first time in my football-following life, I thought I was going to die.

Then one of the lads' girlfriends walks through these right-wing nutters, screaming. I'm thinking, *don't come over to me, fuck off, go away, there's nothing I can do*. But of course, she sees me and comes over bawling, as if Tony O'Neill is going to jump up and save the day. Well, not on this occasion. I grab her, put her on my knee, tell her not to worry and shield my head on her chest. She is asking for her boyfriend but I know he's alright because I can see what's happening.

I sat there for thirty seconds with my head buried in her tits, thinking, *shut up*. Glasses, bottles, bins and chairs are still flying through the air and windows are going through. I get the bird in the café out of the way and sit there with my back to the door, hoping they don't come over. And then as soon as it had started, it was over. As one, the Croatian nutters all moved off together and fucked off back into the dark.

The police turn up but everyone is all right, only one with a small cut behind the ear. Our problem then was that after a quick check the police fucked off and left us – and we still had to get back towards the city centre, which was the very direction the skinheads had gone. We all made it back, but it was an eye-opener to what was to come.

I sat in the hotel with a couple of lads and all these Croatians were looking in the windows for the English and making signs of throats being cut. I had the black eye and the skinhead haircut and the scars on my head, so I wasn't exactly inconspicuous. Some people had managed to get cabs and get out of town to a nightclub, so in the end I did the same. There was a police van outside because the cops were protecting the door. Once inside I just got bladdered, because I knew what kind of place I was in, a nutty place, a nutty city, and with no firm of United lads to speak of, and it was on top, so the only thing to do was get shitfaced.

At some point these big doormen say, 'It is nice to see you but tomorrow you die. It is football.'

A few more brandies go down and we get back at 4 a.m. No problem.

At dinner-time the next day I can see these fuckers walking around again. By now I have learned that they call themselves the Bad Blue Boys, and they are fucking bad. Apparently some people believe the break-up of Yugoslavia actually began at Dynamo Zagreb in 1990, when the Serb lunatic known as Arkan led a mob of 3,000 Red Star Belgrade fans there. The two mobs started throwing stones and seats at each other, and what happened next has been called the worst hooligan riot ever. Thousands of fans fought on the pitch, with even some of the players joining in, and it was only seventy minutes later, when armoured vehicles actually rolled onto the field, that they stopped. A year later, the hostilities broke into civil war and the rest is history.

When you have lived through a war, and most probably fought in it, seen people killed and maybe killed people yourself, it must do something to you. You could see these cunts had been in the army, they were mad, strutting around, going into bars, looking for any English. But United weren't about in big groups – they seemed to have got into the city in two and threes – and I'll give these blokes their due, I think they were looking for our thugs, not normals.

Eventually it kicked off in the town. They had found some kids from Belgrade who had come to support United and had butchered them. I get more beer down me, have a lie down, wake up and come back down into the bar looking for my mate. 'He's in bed and he's paralytic, out of his head,' someone said. I thought, *fuck it, if I'm going to the game, he's coming with me.* So I went and dragged him out.

There were 2,000 soldiers on duty when I got out of the taxi, to protect 400 United fans. The atmosphere outside was so evil it was unreal. I was relieved to get in that ground and more relieved that the police kept us in for a while at the end. Relief turned to joy when I came out and there was a taxi right there. I dived in and got into that hotel and that was where I stayed all night. I think we were lucky there was no firm of United lads because I think we would have all been killed.

I got to find out more about them later and they are anti anyone; they are like a right-wing political party. Theirs was the ground where Arkan from Red Star and his mob had charged in with iron bars, trying to take their end – and he later led a death squad in Bosnia. That was how vicious that place is and it is more political than to do with football. It was the fear of knowing what could happen.

Chapter Twelve

AWAYDAYS

In the 2000–1 season, Manchester United and City had two of the worst records in the country for football violence. United would see 150 soccer-related arrests and City 148, the third and fourth highest in the Premiership, in a season when arrests generally at football increased by eight per cent. 'What became called the English disease is no longer characterised by the mass terrace affrays and running battles we saw in the 1970s and 80s,' said NCIS chief Bryan Drew. 'But, like other infections, new strains of football hooliganism are developing that are clever, resilient and increasingly resistant.' His biggest concern was the hooligans' embracing of communications technology such as mobile phones and Internet to plan confrontations and goad each other. It could equally, however, work against them.

STEVE BARNES: City games always saw big rumbles, obviously. We had big meetings at Chester House involving A Division in the city centre and the two football divisions to co-ordinate our operations for derby matches. United had the major reputation at the time; I think a lot of the City boys were still banned. It was invariably the mass walk from Piccadilly down Oxford

Road. City were usually in pubs and United would walk past and there would be mass bottle throwing and punches and fights. It was always a hard one to police because there were so many people out.

After the game was even worse because they would inter-mingle at the final whistle and then be at it for hours after the game. I remember working some nights in Manchester late on when they would go to the Moon Under Water and would get information where City were and would attack them. We would be in radio contact with their spotters and we'd be running around trying to pre-empt the trouble and stop pubs being smashed up and ordinary people being terrorised.

TONY: How Manchester City are looked upon as the enemy has changed over the years. They are now seen as dangerous not because of their violence but because they will send you to jail. They don't seem to have a clue about the police or CCTV and even film themselves in a fight. They filmed themselves attacking a pub full of Stockport County fans and their own evidence was used to send them to jail. This is the world of fuckwits who try to glamorise football violence and haven't got a clue. They are also filming themselves coming and going to grounds, which they did at Old Trafford once, but unfortunately they had to run off, so that probably spoiled the picture. Why they are so stupid as to allow this to happen is beyond me.

One night they attacked some United lads who had gone out for a drink in the city centre after a game. City had their little spies out hovering around waiting for United lads and went on a building site to get steel poles. They attack this small group of United and at first it was on top for the lads, but in the end they manage to wrestle a metal pole off one of them and turn the tables. In the end, City ran off all the way down Market St. Once again it was all caught on CCTV, because City had attacked them in an area with loads of cameras. That's why some of the United fans didn't move – they knew they could be lifted after if they were seen to be aggressors.

It's normal for the two sides to clash even when they haven't even played each other. In August 1999, we were away at Everton on a Sunday for a late afternoon kick-off and City were at home. Nothing untoward happened at Everton, we got the train, into the pub and then off to the ground under escort. After the game was the usual shite of piling out into the street and trying to get away from the coppers and trying to fuck the Everton off on the corner of Stanley Park, which we did without coming to blows.

We're rounded up and marched back to Lime Street, put on the train and the mood is subdued, nothing to talk about until, twenty minutes from Piccadilly, the phone calls start. City are waiting, a couple of hundred and it's their mob. Well, we can't believe it – but after a few more calls we ascertain it's true. We decide to get off at Oxford Road to attempt to get from there to Piccadilly on foot, hoping the police don't stop us.

They didn't stop us – there weren't any. We thought they'd be there in force before the two mobs could clash but there was no sign of them. We marched across town, cutting through as many side roads as possible, avoiding the main roads, and eventually broke into a canter across the car park of Minshull Street Crown Court. Opposite was a back alley leading to the bottom of Piccadilly.

Now this is one hell of a scene. I'm stood looking round the corner, with a firm of 150 lads all stood waiting for my signal to attack. They can't see how many City there are or who the faces are, but I can see City all in the street, having poured out of the Goose pub full of beer and bouncing about with bottles and glasses in their hands, looking towards the train station. This brought a smile to my face as I thought, in a minute you're in for a right shock. I also thought this could be nasty if I didn't time it right; it could go proper pear-shaped.

They were now spread all over the road, but I could see some of them were baffled, as we hadn't come down the Approach, even though our train had now been in for a good few minutes. It was becoming clear to some of them that something was wrong. I was still observing them, waiting to give the signal, when a couple caught sight of me. They weren't sure what was going on, but they must have sensed rather than known that others were in the side street.

Timing is everything. At that moment we charged out of the side street and caught the vast bulk of them unawares. They were only twenty feet away and by the time they realised and started lobbing their bottles we were into them and smashing those we got to first. City didn't stand, they were scrambling over each other and pulling one another to get back into the pub. There must have been 150 running away in all directions and a few bodies had been slapped silly. We were on their backs as they tried to get in the pub, with loads of them screaming. This was pure football violence and we were loving it even better as it was City and they had thought they'd catch some United on their way home and take liberties. Well, that didn't happen. This was City's firm and they were done in.

Once we had finished them off in the doorway, a few things were being chucked out at us and a few gobs inside the doorway with chairs made a show, but it was too little, too late, as the sirens were heard. But not before they came out and tried to have a go. So one last charge was made at the door to let them know who was boss and back in they went, minus one mug who came out too far and forgot his mates had already run two minutes before. He copped an unopened can of beer full in the face, so hard that the beer exploded out of it. Down he went and we were off, job done.

There were a few little scuffles with stragglers on the way but nothing to worry about and we headed to our own drinking den all laughing, especially about the exploding can, even though it made us shudder at the thought of it. Whoever the guy was, I hope he has given up the hooligan game, and the fact is that no matter how brave he was, he has to remember that those around him weren't. Who needs friends like that?

Just to cheer my City brothers up with a tale of woe, I will confirm the time I came a cropper in a scuffle with them. It was a booze-filled day after a derby at Old Trafford in about 2001. Nothing had gone on, even though a few of us had been up and down Oxford Road and around the university area after the game and had a good drink. On our way back we bumped into fifty City. The usual happened: they threw bottles at us and then we were into them. The battle spread over several streets and we were constantly on the attack until we reached the side streets near the canals in Manchester city centre.

It went off again on a corner and spilled into another side street, where I traded punches with two kids. A third one came running from behind me and landed one on me, proper. My head went. The lad carried on running and the other two went as well, and in a rage I was after them. Without thinking, I left the rest of my lads and went charging off on a solo mission.

I burst out of this side street into the light and suddenly realised I was on my own. This group of City also realised it and slowly came towards me. I had a choice: to run or to stand. I quickly thought about it and decided to stand, more out of tiredness from the ale than anything else, while the thought of running and still getting trampled on and booted to fuck without fighting back did not appeal to me. So I held onto the wall with one hand as they charged into me.

I took a few whacks but not many, as there were too many of them trying to smash down on my head and they were in each other's way. They pushed each other into me and I rolled over on the floor but immediately jumped up and managed to whack the first one. They swarmed all over me again, and again I was bundled over. This time I knew my lives had been used up. I managed to pull away and get off down the street, and they didn't follow. So there I was, stood alone on a street corner with my nose pouring blood all over my coat and feeling pretty sore. I was not a pretty sight, but I knew how lucky I was and that it could have been a lot worse, so I was not too downhearted and things began to look brighter, especially now as the riot van full of coppers went past me.

The passenger side window is down and I can see them all grinning, knowing I've just been done in.

'Everything all right, Mr O'Neill,' shouts one of them.

They are proper taking the piss but I don't let them get to me.

'Some times you have good days and sometimes you have bad days,' I reply. 'No problem, officers. See you later.'

I walked back into town, cleaned myself up in a pub toilets and carried on boozing in a club until 3 a.m. and some of the lads weren't happy when they saw me. It took a while for me to explain to them not to go looking for the City, as they would probably get nicked, and anyway it didn't matter that I had been done, I was okay and had enjoyed my night, so forget it. 'That's what it's all about,' I said. 'Enjoyment.'

The lads weren't happy as it was the first time some of them had seen me like that for a long time and one or two hadn't seen it at all, but as I explained, that's what it's all about. But fuck me, the next morning after waking up on the settee, my head, my arse and my back were proper aching. I was fucked, especially when my missus saw me. All I got from her was, 'You've been done in by City, you stupid old bastard, can't you see you're too old? Even the kids think you're daft.'

With that, it was a quick change of clothes and wash and out of the house down to the Crown pub in Northenden where there were happier faces to mix with and within a few hours the beer was flowing and the aches and pains were gone. Happy days were back.

I miss Maine Road now they're at their new stadium. Going there for us lads was always a pleasure, something we miss with all those dodgy back alleys. It was great – but only if you went mobbed up.

———————

Between 2000–2 the National Criminal Intelligence Service tracked the activities of United's firm. A selection of the reports they compiled indicates how active the gang was:

29 January 2000
Manchester United v Middlesbrough

A group of 50 Middlesbrough supporters arrived in Manchester at 11am. They then went to a city centre pub. At 11.15 a.m. this group was attacked by around 150 Manchester United supporters. Large-scale disorder broke out resulting in damage to the public house and several injuries to those involved in the fighting. No complaints were made to the police by any of those involved in the disorder. Extra police officers attended the scene and dispersed the Manchester United supporters.

1 October 2000
Arsenal v Manchester United

150 Manchester United known hooligans travelled by train to London. This group made their way to the Holloway Road area, eventually increasing their numbers to 200. No disorder occurred before the match due to large numbers

of police. After the game the two hooligan groups were monitored along Drayton Park to the Holloway Road. Once they both realised there were only a few police officers present they charged at each other. Batons were drawn and order was restored. The Manchester United group was corralled and taken to Euston. Over 50 of this group alighted at Watford Junction and caused problems all evening in Watford. They eventually caught the last train to Manchester. This group caused disorder on the train with passengers being abused and sprayed with fire extinguishers. Two females were indecently assaulted.

14 October 2000
Leicester City v Manchester United

The Manchester United main group stopped off at Derby for a drink and did not arrive at Leicester until 2.30pm. Pre-match was quiet although the Leicester group was waiting at the station for Man United to arrive. Post match the Leicester group was waiting at the station for Man United to arrive back and when they did, Leicester stormed out of local pubs and disorder occurred including bottles, bricks and coins thrown at police. The Leicester group then tried to enter the rear of the station but were repelled by police. Only prompt police action prevented major disorder occurring.

21 October 2000
Manchester United v Leeds United

After this fixture a large group of Manchester United supporters made their way to Stockport. This group, numbering over 100 attacked police officers with glasses and bottles before being dispersed. Five arrests were made.

4 November 2000
Coventry City v Manchester United

Prior to this fixture a group of 50 Coventry supporters were drinking at a local public house. Six Manchester United supporters managed to get into the pub and disorder broke out. Police entered and managed to get the Manchester United supporters out. Further disorder broke out involving approximately 50 Coventry and 80 Manchester supporters. Police attended and separated the rival groups. After Manchester United scored the first goal disorder broke out inside the stadium. Just after half time a man ran onto the pitch and play had to be stopped until stewards removed him. After the match a group of 50 Manchester supporters were escorted from the stadium to a local pub. Disorder broke out in the street with bottles and glasses being thrown. Police drew and used their batons. One male received a leg injury during the disorder. The Manchester supporters were pushed back in the direction of the city centre. They grouped again by the ring road and then headed into the city centre and housed themselves in a pub. Coventry supporters then attempted to get to this pub. A police cordon was placed across the road and the Coventry group was forced back. At 6pm the group from Manchester (approx 120) were escorted to the railway station with no further incidents taking place. They were then put on a train out of Coventry.

17 December 2000
Manchester United v Liverpool

A coach containing Liverpool supporters was stopped by police and taken to a secure area where a police search was enforced. As a result of the search a large number of weapons were recovered from the floor of the coach including Stanley knives, iron bars, ammonia sprays, knuckle-dusters and CS gas sprays disguised as pens. An amount of drugs was also recovered. When the stadium was checked at the end of this fixture 150 seats in the visitors' section of the stadium were found to have been damaged.

30 December 2000
Newcastle United v Manchester United

150 Manchester fans travelled by train for this fixture. A further group of 60 fans travelled from Hartlepool. West Yorkshire police and rail staff at Huddersfield and Castleford ejected 22 fans from trains for disorderly behaviour and ticket offences. The Manchester fans remained on the rail network until 11.15pm. At 7.25pm 15 Manchester United fans entered the buffet on York station and stole a quantity of alcohol.

13 January 2001
Bradford City v Manchester United

Intelligence for this fixture indicated that Manchester and Leeds fans had planned disorder at Halifax. After disturbances in Halifax the Manchester fans travelled by train to Bradford. As some Manchester fans used mob tactics to avoid paying fares all season a barrier check aided by police was set up at Bradford and over £1000 was collected. After the match Leeds fans again started grouping and it became obvious that disorder was planned. All the Manchester fans were placed on the train back to Manchester and police on board ensured that they did not get off en route to prevent disorder. This operation was an example of an excellent policing plan between BTP areas and two other forces whereby the policing tactics used on the day prevented major disorder.

During this game rival supporters clashed with each other inside the stadium. Several fights erupted and there was spitting and verbal abuse between the supporters. Several arrest were made. At the end of the match there were sporadic outbursts of fighting between the rival groups. A section of the Manchester United supporters made their way to the city centre. This group fought with anyone who challenged them on route. As the Manchester group passed through Centenary Square individual fights occurred between rival groups.

21 April 2001
Manchester United v Manchester City

Prior to the game, around 150–200 City supporters were located in a public house 2–3 miles away from the stadium. The majority of the group were escorted to the stadium and arrived after kick-off and there were therefore no confrontations between the two groups prior to the kick-off. A number of City supporters were however arrested on their way to the stadium for public order offences and around 30 were refused entry to the stadium as they did not have tickets. They then made their way back to the public house. City fans were kept in the stadium after the game, negating the chance for incidents of disorder in the stadium. The City supporters then regrouped in the pub they had been in prior to the game. The United group appeared shortly thereafter and disorder broke out resulting in a number of arrests. The groups then moved into the city centre where several attempted confrontations were prevented by police. The City group then attacked a public house containing around 40 United supporters. Windows were damaged and missiles thrown, resulting in further arrests. Later in the evening there were a number of running battles and further arrests were made.

January 29, 2002
Bolton Wanderers v Manchester United

A tense stand-off developed in Bolton town centre before the match. More than 40 Manchester United fans gathered in Corks Pub while Bolton supporters packed into Yates Wine Lodge across the road. 60 police officers in riot gear blocked off the road and used eight police vans to form a cordon down the middle of the road. Two of Corks' windows were smashed and bottles and glasses were thrown as the hooligan groups tried to get at each other. There were 20 arrests and 20 more fans were ejected from the Reebok stadium during the game.

30 March 2002
Leeds United v Manchester United

Rival football fans clashed outside the ground following the Premiership match at Elland Road. Eight men were arrested for various offences including public disorder and being drunk and disorderly but police managed to prevent major disorder.

TONY: Bradford City away could go down as the longest day for fighting. We were all meeting at 11 a.m. to get a train to Bradford. All the lads. Before I knew it there was about forty of us. Then we were told by Wing, through a ticket tout called Fat Tony, that we were getting off at Rochdale because Leeds were there and as Fat Tony knows Leeds fans he made sure that info was right. Not that Fat Tony was with us. Leeds were travelling through on their way to play City at Maine Road. We got the train and made sure it was stopping at Rochdale but the police don't know we are getting off at Rochdale as there is no police presence there.

We were checking all the boozers along the way into the town centre from the train station. Then the shout went up that they were in Yates's. In the end the pub was attacked by the first few that got there, with Leeds just charging to the back of the pub, but the disorder was quickly quelled as two vanloads of coppers got there quick. But Leeds shit it, about two coachloads of them. They weren't aware of us coming, that was obvious. We didn't know who these Leeds fans were but we were directed to them by Fat Tony.

Now we are on our way on the train to Bradford. We got off at Bradford late and the police were playing, 'Where's your tickets?' So it was chaos. After a while the police took us to the ground. Unbelievably they put United in two different parts of the ground, which is one of the stupidest things I have ever seen at football. We make our way to the far section where they have a corner section and little scuffles have been going on before we got there. The police are not on this at all. They don't realise there are loads of lads in both ends. There is lots of verbal and then a couple of lads are leaning over and fighting. Then one of the Cockneys dives over into their side of the ground and starts fighting.

It was Bradford's biggest day so they were all out. The game is just about to finish and we come out and there is about 200 of us turn left and are going back round the ground down the street. It is dark and we see a mob coming up the road and we think it is Bradford and we are made up. Turns out it is only the other half of our lads coming up the road. Luckily we clocked this before we got into each other.

Then we come to a junction and Bradford are there. These

cunts have not got a chance. They were all standing at the bottom of this junction with hundreds of nutters running down the road at them in the dark, mostly dressed in black. But let me tell you, half of these cunts stayed to get their heads kicked in. They did not run off at the sight and you have got to give half these kids credit. They stood. They didn't stick together but some of them took it like a man, so to speak.

I copped the first one and he has taken a flying headbutt and he was knocked out before he touched the ground. A few of them got proper slapped and kicked while the others ran off into side streets. From then on the coppers were flying everywhere. There were mobs of twenty to thirty, forty to fifty, running in all directions to try to get Bradford while they were trying to get back together. We were having it with groups of them and it was a proper brawl and Bradford kept coming back and attacking the groups and it was great. Then back to the station. We were talking to some of the coppers on horses and they'd come all the way from Blackpool.

We got on the train and got to Manchester, got off at Victoria and City are all around Shambles Square. There is only one place we are heading. Next thing, we are having them all over the place. There are about 100 City in that area and we all came off, marched up the road behind the Cathedral, through the side streets, little groups of City here and there, and chase them everywhere. Then we just left them, scuttling off. Then we all descended to enjoy the pubs. Stayed in a couple of pubs and all got blind drunk on the longest day of fighting. We were all knackered by that time. It was like the Seventies all over again. Oh what fond memories.

Going to Leicester by train with a lot of lads, our intention was to go into the city centre and get into some boozers. No pre-match arranged meet or anything just a normal day out, but when I think of a normal day out there really isn't such a thing.

THE MEN IN BLACK

The plod try and keep hold of us. This gets everyone off running here and there trying to get away, which a lot of us do by going over a bridge at the bottom of the platform. We run across the car park outside, into the city centre and straight in a boozer, followed by phone calls to tell where we are at, and twenty minutes later most of us are there. So are the plod and a group of Leicester walking back and forth showing their faces.

Beer is consumed for a few hours and then the police close the pub down and have us out on the street and try to keep order. But this military style is only having an effect on the locals, who come out of the bars nearby and go through a ritual which is played up and down the country by so many mongs of shouting abuse like, 'I'll fucking have you, twat, you're fucking dead later.' This only gives the police an excuse to play this game, so the truncheons are out and a few get twatted because they refuse to walk away. Obviously as the saying goes, if it wasn't for the coppers you'd be dead. Well not on this occasion.

The march to the ground is uneventful and outside we hang about, as it is too early to go in at 2.15. We loiter around and the police disappear somewhere else. We start to notice a few unfamiliar faces and then it's obvious that Leicester have made this their biggest day as you now get some walking past giving it the mouth. The first one gets it straight to the side of his head and bang, he's down. Then there is panic as a few more punches are thrown in their direction and this is where I see Mr Shithouse with his ponytail and glasses. He walks up thinking he's one of the boys but as soon as it goes he's the first to scream and he's making sure the plod hear and see him. How many wankers like that have I seen.

Anyway, plod are now running all over and there's no more of it all through the game – although we'll have to be on our toes after the game, as we can feel the hatred towards us. So game over, out we come and get together and instead of going direct into the side street where the police want us to go, we go left.

Slowly we set off, 200 of us, and pass the side streets to our left and right with the straight-member Leicester fans avoiding us. Surprisingly the police were slow off the mark and hadn't dealt with our group, so we all knew it was going to happen. You could see small gangs going backwards as they see us coming. There was no noise, no screaming from us, we knew where we were going and that was to the bottom of the street and down the main road.

This is where they would all be waiting, as their pub is just behind the houses and a lot of them would have stayed there during the match. As we neared you could see them bouncing about on the opposite side of the road, with a few groups on the corner of the street. We kept the walk for as long as we could but the excitement and tension was too much and the charge was full on down the side street. Those few who stood on the corner were butchered as the mob rolled over them and into the road, where now we are into the main Leicester mob and backing them down onto the grass area and forcing them towards the houses. Everyone was punching and kicking and Leicester could not stop us. Yes, they tried but they were on a loser. The police were now charging about trying to split us up so we were now on opposite sides of the road and heading towards town, but not before more skirmishes broke out.

The only problem for me at this time was the Inspector, who had drawn his truncheon and decided that if he was going to use it then I was the one who needed it. So for about 300 yards my back, arms and legs were twatted anytime we made a move. I eventually had to call time on it, as this Inspector didn't care whether I was doing anything or not. I was getting it.

Once across another crossroads and the field to our left, it became orderly and everyone was satisfied with a good day's work. The only thing wrong was this Inspector, who was ordering his officers about, threatening everyone who was in ear blast. He had got carried away with all the aggro and couldn't calm down. Even when we reach the station, he still wants to whack people while we go onto the platform. My shoulder cops another blow from him, so I have to tell him to stop as there is no fighting and all we are doing is getting our train. He then calms down and starts to apologise, realising that fuck all is happening.

We board the train and I'm having a smoke out of the window and we move off. The Inspector is stood there and I bid him farewell and thank him for a lovely day out. He smiles at me and says, 'See you next year Tony,' and we both laugh.

Some days of 'going out', as I put it, are etched in my memory as great adrenalin rushes, and one of them was another Midlands game, at Coventry. It typified what can happen to any United fan who just wanders around thinking after a game he can go for a pint, as twenty of us did.

Leaving the ground, we made our way back to the railway station and kept away from the plod, who were keeping close to the main group of the lads heading into town. We had ducked into a little bar on the road just before where a building overhangs the road. It was small and no-one was in it, so we settled ourselves down and made a few calls to wind up the others, as they were being harassed by the plod who were trying to get them out of town.

An hour had gone by when we noticed a few lads walk past, then a few more. It was obvious to us they were at it, looking for stragglers. These were some of Coventry's finest looking to take liberties and they thought they had found their target.

The pub was small but had large windows and we could see everything, so we started to prepare ourselves. Slowly the coats were back on. No panic, just a few butterflies as it seemed we were outnumbered and it was going to be an all-out assault on us. It was, I thought, a backs-to-the-wall job. They started coming into the passageway to the front door but we could see that some were holding back. So I make the move to the exit door and tell everyone to get ready. We were going out. Those lads with me would hold their hands up as it probably wasn't the wisest move, but what the fuck is it all about? Anyway, if it came on top we could always run back in.

I bolted the exit open and smash! The first one gets a bottle over his head without knowing where it came from. Now they are the ones surprised as we are into them. We've got a couple to our left who try to retreat to the group hanging back, but they have no chance and are smashed in the first attack.

It's now onto this second group, who have been held at bay with the help of a couple of chairs and bottles. We go flying into them and they are scattering all over the road. Straight away I've got one and sent him flying but fair play to the lad, he tries to rally his pals. Unfortunately for him Bucket is on him again and he gets several whacks, which put him down and out.

His pleas haven't helped him, as his mates scatter all over the roads when they see him go down and start to run off. The funny thing about it all was, we then went back in the pub, asked the landlord if he was alright, explained to him that it wasn't our fault and said if we hadn't gone out his bar would have been wrecked. He was okay about it and he was on our side, so when the plod do turn up everything is sweet. We finish our beer and then are taken up to town to join all the others, who have been cornered into a pub near the station and are gutted at having missed out.

Coventry's lads were looking for divs that day, something that goes on a lot against United fans. Another place where that went on was Sunderland, when they first came back up to the Premier League. We went up there for a night game on a couple of coaches. Stopped before we got there, met a few other people, had a few beers, a half-decent bunch of lads and off we go again on the coaches and come into Sunderland where the main iron bridge is. We pull up, having gone past a lot of pubs. We are just before the bridge and all piling off. We are just getting on the bridge and there are Sunderland lads there. I have just got off the lead coach and a couple of Sunderland boys are in my face. They weren't sure if we were lads or not. Next thing, I blasted this kid on the bridge, knocked him down and went for his pal. There was a group of them but they fucked off.

The police came from behind and got everyone but about eight of us crossed over and got to the other side of the bridge. There was a subway and I thought, I have been too smart for my own good here because there was a few of them bouncing about, ten or fifteen of them, younger lads. So we go towards them, they want it, we go into them and they run off.

But no way was I going under that subway. We come back up and cross the road. This was beginning to look right on top. We are now in two and threes because they are coming out of the boozers onto the street. We carry on and no-one bothers us. We get to the ground but most haven't got tickets.

Sunderland come round the corner but we all end up in the ground. The police also bring the coaches right outside the turnstiles.

After the game there is all the usual shouting and bawling in the dark, some minor scuffles – and that was it. But it was a mad area that reminded me of the 70s, people running around, the police looking like they have it under control but not really.

Next time we play them away there is no firm going up, it is another night game and I have gone with my pals in a seven-seater. We stop a couple of minutes away from the ground, have a meal and a drink and you get a free bus ride from the park-and-ride place. We join the queue with all these Sunderland from the park-and-ride, no problem, get the bus and then walk through to United's end. There's a little bit of verbal outside but nothing much.

We come out at the end, go to the left, we are not walking together but we know where we are going. There were six of us, and fuck me, it came right on top. This typifies the hatred towards United. There's only half a dozen of us but I have had to put my back to the wall of the ground because the scream has gone up and all Sunderland are pressing towards us. We can't go anywhere, left or right, all we can do is take a stance and wait for it. All attention seems to focus on us. They were threatening us and mingling round trying to get near us.

One kid comes by my side with his cap on, coat zipped up, all that bollocks, and I'm waiting for the sly dig when the coppers turn away. I didn't want to smack anyone but I had no choice, and smash, threw a quick right hand right in his face – and it turns out he was a United fan. He just fucked off after I smacked him but it made the roar go up even louder and now they all wanted to kill us. We were there for twenty minutes, couldn't move.

The police told us to get in the back of a cop van. We were prevaricating, thinking it wasn't right, one or two wanted to get in but then my pal said, 'No, we can't get in there, it's not right.' So we said no, we were getting the park and ride bus as soon as the coast was clear. Eventually it calmed down but there were still a few of them hanging around watching us. A couple of police at first stay with us but then let us go because it is now half an hour after the game and we are still on the corner. We walk off and a couple in the car park start following.

This big bastard bowls over, pissed, saying, 'Munich cunts.' We whip round the car to cut him off and blast him and he scrambles away. But a couple of others keep following at a distance.

We join the park and ride line but these tricky cunts have now got a couple of their pals. They start giving us abuse and trying to wind up people in the queue to attack us, but the other people aren't having it. I said, 'We're going to have to get off here and get away from this place before they get people at it.' We start to move off and suddenly they all start screaming and moving towards the six of us.

These are typical north-east football hooligans, a rabble, and I have found myself in a situation loads of straight members have been in, going back to a car park, not knowing anything, and being singled out for attack by a pack. We end up having to run up a slip road to get away from the queue but these mongs think we are running from them, so they run after us. We stop in the road and pick up some missiles. They stop but carry on giving us abuse.

There is a pub on the slip road. We can't stop and have it with these lads because if we don't get off this slip road the pub will empty and we'll be fucked. We carry on walking and this time they don't follow. We have to walk along the dual carriageway all the way back. It goes to show you can't just follow your team because you take your life in your hands from liberty-takers like that.

We get back to this bar and there is a club in Newcastle, owned by a friend's relative. A few phone calls are made and we end up at this club. We go in, the same six, and we are sectioned off and get absolutely bladdered. I turn up at 8:30 a.m. at my office with my missus going mental. I had to explain to her that we'd been delayed overnight because of terrible fog all the way back. It didn't go down well and that was another two days without a cooked meal.

A United fan coming out of Tottenham's ground minding his own business, a Spurs fan comes up and smashes him in the face and runs off and he winds up in hospital with a broken jaw. United fan outside Upton Park, young lad, gets slashed. A United fan at Middlesbrough, a normal bloke, walking back and your big Boro fan, in his baseball hat, smashes him in the head and the bloke collapses on the floor. What do they get out of that? I don't get it, but that is the hatred towards United. What is in the minds of these plums?

Chapter Thirteen

SUPERFIRM

BY NOW SOME hooligans had taken to referring to United's mob as the Superfirm. Partly this was because of their continued successes against other gangs on trips away, partly because of their 'gangster' connections, and partly the belief that their numbers had been bolstered by recruits from other clubs, in particular a heavy mob from the Edinburgh side Hibernian.

TONY: We had a lad, Spence, who was well-known at Oldham and started coming to United. He was typical of what I would call the new breed: get everywhere, know everyone, always on the mobile phone, running around following England and visiting other clubs. One of our lads, who was similar in a way, brought him along and this eventually led to half a dozen Hibs coming through with Spence. They were handy lads in their own right. People started to call United the Superfirm but it was only half a dozen lads, not like the Chelseas of this world who have loads of hangers-on. This Hibs firm even ended up bringing their kids to the games.

In the Eighties, most we won, some we lost, but the Nineties was mainly the Men In Black going about doing the business. The last truly big row we had was in Leeds on 3 March 2001, when the MIB ran riot after the game and smashed the Yorkies all over on a housing estate called Holbeck. That was the last free-for-all.

The police had the train station covered when United arrived and we were placed on buses and taken to the ground. As I said in *Red Army General*, the police at Leeds are useless and this day was no different. If you are kept in after the game for twenty minutes, you would think that when you come out the buses would be there waiting to take you back.

Well you've guessed it, no buses, so you have Leeds down the road giving it the big one and the police saying nothing to United fans as they make their way home. We are on our way to the train station. The police have no idea what to do with us and quickly lose control. After a few skirmishes we head across the roundabout trying to make our own way to the city centre, which obviously gives us the chance to take it to Leeds if they fancy it.

We eventually are met by some high fencing which stops us progressing, but a hole is found in the fence and people duly queue up in an orderly fashion, get through it and make their way across some fields to Holbeck estate. Then people hear a roar. They can't see anything but they can hear it. They charge down this slippery bank and everyone is following and now they can see all the lads in front fighting. Leeds are trying to force their way down but the lads are standing firm.

Before I go on I must explain that the fighting that went on led to some arrests in dawn raids. Fortunately for a lot of the lads, the police were slow to act, as it was their lack of organisation which let the Leeds mob attack us on our way back to the station. We were well aware of hundreds of Leeds scampering across the bridge over the motorway where more Leeds were gathered and they came charging towards one of the alleyways where the first group of United lads stood, well outnumbered.

JB: After the game, police were everywhere, but the buses they were trying to put us on had moved, so there was confusion. We did a left and fucked off, walking down the dual carriageway. A main Cockney Red says, 'Come this way,' and there was a fence with a hole in. We ducked through the hole and slipped down this embankment and others must have seen us and followed. It's a bit wet and muddy and my main preoccupation is not getting shit on me.

Three of us came between these houses and there's ten or fifteen lads facing us. They shout, 'Munich are here!'

We engage them straight away and then more people come behind me and it has gone big time. Leeds are coming through with pieces of wood and twatting us. There's a copper filming it from a motorway bridge, and a helicopter hovering overhead, but more and more come and we battle like fuck and drive them back to this passageway beside these houses.

An old lady came out and said, 'What are you doing in my garden?'

They must have come behind us but by then the next United firm is there and it is going everywhere. There's lads getting whacked with fence posts. I picked up a bit of fencing, then realised the helicopter was overhead and dropped it. The only people to get charged were those with weapons in their hands from the helicopter film.

TONY: They never moved United from the alleyway and all the time the rest, nearly all dressed in black, were charging across the field to join in. Suddenly people were brawling in gardens and everything from chairs and wheelie bins to planks of wood and even a vacuum cleaner was being thrown. Within a minute

Leeds were being smashed up the alley and running off, but one of their lads is stood there and he's not moving. He takes full hit, one arrow, and he's down unconscious with the mob trampling over him. And all the time United were fucking Leeds off. About seventy United ran down this road and saw them off, then as they came back, the kid who'd been hit is walking around in a circle not knowing where he was and he ends up getting twatted again.

After a few minutes, United were all back together when Leeds came up from a side street and at the same time came from behind some pub on the estate. One firm charged down the street and smashed into Leeds who again were running off, and it was only the police on horses who kept us from finishing them off.

Now that firm rejoined the other group, who had chased the rest of the Leeds back behind the pub, and off we went. Leeds had been done in, all on Holbeck estate; there was no escaping that fact. The firm was buzzing as this had been something the police had, in effect, let happen, even though their records say it was planned. They would say that, wouldn't they?

It was like the old days and all the young ones who were there with us could not believe it. They took delight in sharing the feeling of the good old days when the Red Army went on the rampage. The only difference was this time the police used cameras from a safe distance and a few lads were given prison sentences later on. But ask anyone who was there: doing the time would have been worth it because the buzz was unbelievable. Later on that night the phones were going across to Leeds and they were ill. They had even started arguing and fighting with each other. As I said to Shaun over in Leeds, 'What did you expect?'

THE MEN IN BLACK

POLICE ROUND UP SOCCER THUG SUSPECTS

Football hooligans were the latest targets of West Yorkshire Police's crime crackdown yesterday, when officers staged dawn swoops on homes across the country to arrest suspected troublemakers.

Officers were looking for soccer supporters suspected of being involved in violence after a Leeds United v Manchester United match in March.

The raids were carried out on homes in south Yorkshire, Manchester and North Wales.

Yesterday's operation was launched as part of West Yorkshire Police's Target initiative.

At 7am officers from Holbeck set out and arrested nine men throughout the course of the day, eight of whom had been charged by late last night.

Following the match, which kicked off at 11.30am, disorder broke out in Tilbury View, Holbeck, and surrounding streets.

As many as 50 Leeds and Manchester fans clashed in the streets. Some were armed with sticks and others began throwing sticks and stones.

Fourteen people were arrested at the time and a number have been subsequently charged.

A team of detectives was set up to try to identify others suspected of being involved. The officers have studied hours of film taken by the West Yorkshire Police helicopter and other footage.

It was that investigation which sparked yesterday's raid.

Yorkshire Post, 14 June 2001

___

TONY: Three weeks after the Holbeck incident, England played Finland at Anfield. It's not my scene, but people were saying they were going, and at the end of the day, I'm off. Two hundred and fifty of us meet at Piccadilly Station, all the lads. We arrive at Lime Street, get off and the police are there. Who are they bothered about? Man United. I jib off and have a quick look around and there's people and faces all over the place. They take United out of the city centre. I go with them and we are on our way to the ground. It was 11am when we arrived.

We know where we are going so we plot up in Everton Valley in a couple of pubs where we are joined by more and soon there's about 350 in the two pubs.

That day was typical of the English hoolie bollocks at these games. Everybody hates Man United and they're always going on about what they will do to us. Well that day there were different firms from all over the country and all they did was stay in Liverpool city centre drinking with each other, letting on to each other and avoiding each other. There were loads of phone calls going from certain people to other people in the city centre, telling them exactly where we were. We were there until about 2.30 p.m. Nobody came. Yet you go in Liverpool city centre for an England game and all you have is police. I don't understand why people do that. We didn't: we marched to the ground at 2.30. People were stopping in the street to stare at us and they knew who we were.

Half of us had tickets and half didn't. We had a big block of seats in the main Stand at the back, a big block in the Kop and a block in the Anfield Road End and at no point did anybody say anything to us. A few got slapped for gobbing it, just some pissed cunts saying, 'You're supposed to support England.' Because in the Main Stand we were shouting, 'United.' To be honest it was so boring to sit there and watch other players from other teams, I didn't have the heart to shout encouragement.

Anyway, everyone hates United who goes to those games. You often hear, 'Stand up if you hate Man U.' But nobody that day came near us, including the Scousers.

At half-time we came out because we were bored and all went back boozing to where we had been before because it was crap. We had been expecting chaos. The game finished and we stayed in the two pubs for about twenty minutes, then we were all out on the streets. The police gave us one of the biggest escorts I have ever had. They contained us on Scotty Road and marched us all the way back to the platform at Lime Street. How can you get an escort when you are supposed to be England fans and the home team.

This was where I realised it was all coming to an end. Things were starting to add up and I thought, *this is crap*. All these so-called top boys of all these so-called top firms, yet the only fighting I heard of that day was the Oldham or Stockport went back towards Everton's ground after the game, attacked a pub and battered a mob of Everton. It was one of those days where things were starting to add up.

JB: We don't normally do England games but because it was Anfield we said we would. We arranged it beforehand, all met up at various points in Manchester, and got the train from Oxford Road. There was a good 250. It was at the time everyone was dressing in black and as we came out of Lime Street near the taxi rank there was police and loads of different firms of England fans everywhere. Everybody just stopped, including the police, to watch us come out of the station. Instead of turning into the town centre we started marching to the ground. No-one acknowledged us, no-one spoke to us, but everyone clocked us. Instantly the police were following us, which they did all the way.

As we got on the main drag near Anfield we started shouting,

'Who the fuck are England?' People were getting slapped and we started loud chants of, 'United.' We couldn't even engage other firms of England to have a go at us, they all gave us a wide berth. It wasn't for want of trying. We saw loads of lads but they never fronted us. The Scousers were conspicuous by their total absence. But then I don't think Liverpool really do England.

We walked round the ground several times. Some of us went in and some went to the pub and coming outside you would think it was a United away game at Liverpool, with all the police around us.

TONY: We played Liverpool at Anfield immediately after the Finland game, and that was when it finally became clear to me that it was over. Week after week, when I go away, I get pressure off the police and put up with it. It is part and parcel. But at that Liverpool game it was right on top for me, in a way that was worse than anything before. Two hundred and fifty of us had been there the week before, the following week there was thirty of us. And there we are, a few straight members as well, going past Edge Hill and there the Scousers are, on their mobile phones, telling their mates we are on the train. But when we get to Lime Street the police have got me, dragged me out of the station, got me away from most people and told me straight.

'You think you are fucking coming here like you did last week, thinking you are going to do this and that' – with the occasional little dig thrown in – 'we are going to kick your fucking head in the first time we see you move, say anything, do anything, we are going to fucking leather you.'

I looked at these two as they held me by the throat and they were foaming at the mouth. I knew with the reputation of the Scouse coppers towards us anyway that this was the end of coming to Merseyside. They let me back with the others and led us out and now these two are talking to all the other coppers and pointing to me, saying, 'That's the cunt there.'

To be honest, when I got to the ground I wanted to turn around and go back while I was in the escort, but if I had I would have been leathered. It was the worst ever with the police and yet the smallest mob. I thought, *people are doing other things here. They're not doing these games any more. What is this all about?* Obviously your criminals have better things to do.

We got outside United's end and everyone was mingling about, so I jibbed through the passageway, got off through Stanley Park and went to a pub on my own. I knew not to go in that ground; something bad would have happened. Before the game ended, I made my way back and stood behind the wall. Everyone came out and I was stood offside on my own, watching. Then I joined in and marched back and never said another word. I have not been back to Liverpool since.

---

12 August 2001
Manchester United v Liverpool

Cardiff supporters returning from their league match against Wycombe found the Prince of Wales pub full of Manchester United fans, in town for the Charity Shield the next day. Police kept the two groups apart with drawn batons and the hooligans fought running battles with police through the evening. 22 people were arrested, including two Cardiff youths aged just 11 and 13. One fan was slashed and a police officer suffered a broken arm. There was further violence before the Charity Shield game the next day when eye-witnesses described how a 50-strong

mob of Liverpool and Cardiff fans attacked Manchester
followers in Wood Street.

NCIS report

TONY: Cardiff City had played at our place but their Soul Crew
never came. We know, though, that when we go down there for
the Charity Shield on a Sunday against Liverpool it will be a
different story. We know the Scousers won't turn up in Cardiff
city centre on the Saturday, but there is all the talk and worry of
how do we deal with something we have never encountered
before – half of Wales turning out in their capital city to have a
crack at us.

How are we all going to get there and get together? A group
of us decide to go on the train via Birmingham and Reading.
Cardiff are playing at home on the Saturday so do we get there
after 3 p.m., hoping all the Cardiff are in their ground and
giving ourselves a chance to get our firm together to face them
afterwards, or do we go there early? Well, in for a penny, in for
a pound. No point being there after 3 p.m.

Everybody going down there knows what to expect and
knows that our group is going to land there first at about 1.30.
All the time, I'm thinking, *fuck, there is only a small firm, about
fifty- or sixty-handed, this could come right on top*. We get off at
Cardiff and come out to police with cameras. We get to the
corner and go in the pub. We get our heads together and wait for
it.

Nothing happens for a while. We see a couple of Cardiff
walking past, hanging around. We thought we could hold the
pub, but this is all paranoia of the unexpected. We are getting
phone calls off people saying they will be there in fifteen minutes,
twenty minutes. We come out of the pub at about 3 p.m., go up

203

the road, go in another pub and there are about 150 of us now. We are right in the centre, big pub, the Prince of Wales, and we are having it. By 4 p.m., it is packed full of United. We are firm-handed and it is still early doors. Eventually there are several hundred in there, with loads of police about.

At 5 p.m., Cardiff start coming into town after their game, not very happy at our presence. We are in the pub taking the piss and they are in the street going mad. Some United whip out through the side door, few scuffles, people standing off, then getting whacked, five here, ten there, all having a quick go at each other.

Cardiff are going mental, hatred in their faces, they can't believe we are all there. They know we are taking the piss. All they want to do is storm the pub but the police have blocked off the road. However, some United are still scuttling around the back streets and having a pop. One young firm comes back who've have had it on a corner where it came on top for them. Little tit-for-tats go on for a while and all the time the pressure is building for a major kick-off.

It came to a point where the beer and atmosphere all got too much, the doors were kicked open as the police tried furiously to keep us in, and the whole boozer piled out into the street and tried to get to the main road. But the police managed to trap us all in this side street. This goes on for twenty minutes, cops hitting us, dogs biting people. In the end several hundred of us make a charge the opposite way down this side street and come out not far from the railway station.

We are intercepted by cops and horses but it is chaos. We manage to get back into the city centre but our group ends up being forced to get into cabs and drive out of town by the cops. We wouldn't have lasted long anyway, because everyone was bladdered. Then it was everyone back to the hotels, which we haven't even booked into yet. Our hotel was the Cardiff Bay and next thing the people I'm with are getting phone calls, 'We are in this pub, Poet's Corner.' This is about 8 p.m. So we get in cabs again. All the other United lads scattered about are also getting calls.

When we arrive at the pub, in the back streets of the town, about twenty United lads are in there. It is some local's birthday, a private function with a buffet laid out, but he didn't mind the United fans being there. Well, you give an inch and people take a mile. United are arriving from all directions and soon there is mayhem in this bar.

One police van is parked outside. Someone comes in and says, 'They're here!' I thought it was bollocks but they really were there, a group of Cardiff, and Wing and a few others are outside. They are coming over and they are having it. I get outside and they are fronting it up: 'We're Cardiff, you Man U shite.' It took me back to the old days. Did they really think they could shout at us and look aggressive and we were going to run off? A few of them were walking over thinking we would shit it. The first one came up mouthing when he should have been flying in. He clearly thinks he's ten men.

He gets a bottle smashed over his head and he has gone. Then we are into them. We give it to a couple of them and the cop van with two officers tries to position itself between us but there was none of that, we were all around it. I get behind the van with a few others and we are after the Cardiff but they have gone. They've had the shock of their lives against seasoned pros who are not scared of a bit of shouting.

They are chased down this long street. We manage to trip one up, jump on another one and they get smashed. They are still running when we come to this bridge. The police have driven straight past us and stopped the rest of the United pack from following us, so there's just a few of us left chasing them. I think to myself, *don't push it, if you get caught you're fucked*. I stop but some of the young lads keep going, even though I tell them not to.

More Cardiff pull up over the bridge. The United who had kept chasing them now came charging back; the situation had been reversed. We are on the other side of the road and they come running over to join us, with Cardiff on their heels. I don't know how many Welshmen were coming round this corner but the first three were right big lumps and I was praying there weren't many more like them. But I had to stand, and I knew without anyone having to say it that it was down to me. I knew everyone was waiting for me to do something, and the kids with me would prefer to fuck off because this is on top.

The first big lump comes over, all flying arms, and takes a swing at me. I deck him. More are coming round the corner but the kids I'm with are game now and are in a tight ball. It breaks into scuffles. What saved us was the police coming up the road on foot. It was so dark I hadn't seen them and they arrived without us realising it. They nick a couple and we whip back towards the pub.

We get there and there are now lots of us, 150–200. They march us back to town and we are full of the drink. We get opposite the railway station and go left into the town centre. We want to get there because we are now up for it. The riot police have blocked off the street and are fighting with us to keep us away. It was touch and go, but in the end the police won. Then it was all back to the Cardiff Bay area and a good sing-song in a bar.

Nothing happened the next day except the Scousers went round United's end just before kick-off and attacked a lot of straight members. I think a United fan got slashed but I don't know if that was by Liverpool or Cardiff, and you got Cardiff driving about in cars on the edge of town. But we'd done the job the day before.

Chapter Fourteen

OLD HABITS DIE HARD

THE MEN IN Black knew the writing was on the wall. They couldn't carry on the way they had, yet nor could they kick the habit. They had been active for so long, with such success, that the buzz carried them along, even though the police now knew almost all of their main faces.

That reality was finally driven home to Tony O'Neill on 6 October 2001, the day England were due to play Greece at Old Trafford. Hooligans from all over Britain gathered in the city's pubs, some to go to the match, some just to be there and some to look for a fight. When a mob of United fans arrived at one particular pub, a fight broke out with elements of Stoke City's Naughty Forty and Under-Fives. After a brief ruck in which bottles and ashtrays were thrown, Tony was arrested.

TONY: There was the biggest concentration for an England game of football hooligans ever. There were gangs from every-where. Yet when I went into town, nothing was happening. There were no mob riots. The police had all United fans locked in a big boozer for four hours, forcing them into Salford, forcing them to disperse. I got nicked after going into a pub. There were loads of people in the pub, straight members, hooligans, God knows what. A disturbance breaks out and I'm the only one nicked. That says to me, you are finished. There is a lot more to the story of me getting nicked but it is all bollocks.

I was charged with violent disorder, released on bail and continued going to matches. The following January I went to Aston Villa, which has to be the worst place you can visit for over-reaction by the police towards football fans. Consistently they behave aggressively without provocation. I believe this is at the behest of their so-called football intelligence, something I came across in 2002 when we won 3–2 in the cup after being 2–0 down at half-time. The only trouble was that they didn't give me a chance to see the game, as I was given a good kicking in the car park just before kick-off by four coppers.

As I walked through the car park I was suddenly pulled from behind and asked where I was going. Well, you'd think that outside a football ground two minutes before kick-off, just me and a friend, walking in the direction of the turnstiles, with a ticket in my hand, it was pretty fucking obvious where I was going, but these thugs weren't up for thinking. They had been sent by their hoolie coppers, and ours no doubt, to intercept me.

An argument broke out and I was pulled to the side and ended up behind some vehicles, where they attacked me. This might sound outrageous to some people – and also like sour grapes, coming from me – but let me explain. Us blokes all know how to protect our bollocks, and if we don't it's curtains. Well, as I'm stood upright I see this big lump of a copper and think he's shaping to boot me in the bollocks, but I dismiss the thought, as we are only arguing at that time and it was not heated enough to warrant such an over-reaction.

Suddenly the night sky is rolling about above my head and I'm gasping for air and trying to breathe and let out a scream but nothing comes out. My brain is in shock with the pain. The bastard had caught me full with his size twelve and I mean full. I was down on the floor, being manhandled and told to stop struggling. They were having a laugh; it wasn't a struggle, it was a seizure. My balls were on fire and felt as though they were in my throat. I was proper out of it and felt like crying, this was the worst pain ever inflicted on me. But I think the shock of it, as I wasn't expecting the big lump to do it, made it worse.

All the usual crap happens, arms up my back and dragged off but not before I've had the pleasure of another size twelve firmly planted on my face, which left a tarmac imprint on one side of my kite and his boot sole on the other.

I won't bore you with the details of police procedure for the next couple of hours after my arrest but at about twelve o'clock I'm released. By this time I'm walking funny, my balls feel as though they're on fire and I think I'm carrying the match ball in my jeans. The throbbing is constant and all I want to do is go home but I'm staying put until I've seen the Inspector, as I'm going to make a complaint.

They keep me waiting for another hour until I am escorted into a room where the Inspector tells me to sit down. I thought he was taking the piss, as he could see the discomfort I was in, but that was nothing to what he said after I'd relayed what had happened. He told me that knowing his officers as he did, they were probably using the appropriate force necessary. The twat ignored the fact that I had not been doing anything and then fucked me off when I asked him at what stage of their police training did they learn to use the right boot to restrain prisoners by kicking them in the testicles.

'There's the door,' he replied. 'You can use the payphone for a taxi.'

The taxi arrived and I jumped in with another United fan and paid £95 before we set off. I then had to endure the journey home with the front passenger seat moved forward and my feet resting on top of the seat with my legs apart, my pants down and my balls hanging out so they could have some room and fresh air, as they were still burning up. All I got at home was the usual 'You must have done something', so for the rest of the week I went hungry again as there were no meals cooked for me.

Saturday approaches and Southampton away looked more appealing than being at home, so I'm off, not in the best of condition but a few beers and everything looks rosy. I am now recalling the events of Aston Villa to anyone willing to listen and occasionally get my bollocks out, which are now a very dark purple and a grotesque size. This is all good fun and any thoughts of trouble are at the back of my mind even though I'm in a pub full of Southampton fans.

This pub is next to the estate near the ground and after the game I go back there and quite a few more Reds end up there after a few calls on the phone asking where I am. This is no hoolie mob, it's just lads having a drink. The pub is full and there's a few couples in our group and the same banter as before starts. This goes on for an hour and a half when the mood changes, as outside and inside the pub there are now Southampton lads on mobile phones and eyeing us up.

This is a situation played out hundreds of times across the country wherever United play. Your so-called hoolie now sees United fans drinking in a pub and thinks they're fair game for a hiding. The fact that it's not a hoolie mob does not concern them; we're United fans so we're going to get it. It's funny when you think of all the times you hear these 'lads' spouting off about only fighting those who want it. Pure shite, as some of the best times I have had is when these cunts turn up thinking they've found easy pickings.

In they come, over to where we were stood, and straight away I know it's on me. This big twat comes over first with a few lads behind him but he feels awkward, as no-one acknowledges him. Most of the people try to ignore his presence but I stop him in his tracks with my mouth, saying, 'Look mate, I'm with my missus, we don't want trouble.' He fucks off without a word, leading his pals into the other room and out into the street, where you can see others hanging about.

No-one wants trouble but to me it's obvious that it's going to happen, no matter what, so I explain we either stay in here and get blitzed or we go out and have it with them. I'm going out anyway, as there was really no choice, and everyone else agreed. So out we went.

Standing to my left was the big cunt from the pub. All I can say is, what a bunch of shithouses. I turn to him and say, 'Do you want a fight?' and before he has replied, the glass has landed in his forehead and he's scrambling back into the pub. Every one of those Southampton twats legged it, so we charged at them, with a few getting twatted. A proper bunch of cowards they were; they were looking for victims but we were having none of it.

They have moved ground now and like to hide on that estate nearby and look to pick people off, which they did a few years later: a United fan, who was harmless, was attacked with baseball bats, iron bars, sticks, bottles, bricks, over fifty of them attacking a small group on their way to the ground. The result was the lad lost one-third of his skull. By some miracle he lived but what the future holds for him, God only knows. Now that is not what it is all about.

For twenty years I've had no serious trouble at Southampton, then suddenly they move to a new ground and they think behaving the way they have makes them tough. Well, you pricks, talk to the men of the Seventies. Shame on you all, not even a sign of compassion from any genuine Southampton fans for the plight of this man and his family, but that's the new supporter for you, thank God I don't bother any more.

Football violence as people view it today is the Internet, mobile phones and faces of different clubs knowing each other. It usually ends in farce, and I hate all the bullshit that accompanies it. After thirty years of trying to survive in this world I know bullshit when I see it. As I've said before, if you want fun then just get out of your house and get on a train and get yourself to the town of where you're playing with no plan but whatever happens, happens. With United this was our way on most occasions. It's just a pity a lot of your hoolie gangs don't do the same. Having to keep it organised so you don't get leathered is not what it was all about. To me you went and had fun and if you got leathered, so be it. Getting a Stanley knife or stabbing was not our game. It's just a pity others thought it was.

Funnily enough, I nearly had a fight with the former Chelsea player Peter Osgood when we played a Monday night match at Southampton. He was in a pub opposite the ground with a minder. We were staying the night. About fifteen of us were in there, along with some Southampton fans, and I'm having the crack with them. Osgood is at the bar with his minder and because they had won I was winding them up, saying, 'Well, what have you ever won?' Even though I knew they had won the FA Cup against us.

Osgood jumps off his bar stool as though his head had snapped and bounced over.

'We beat you in the cup final in '76,' he declared.

It took me by surprise because I was only having a laugh. I thought, this cunt wants it. The minder pulls him back and the landlord goes off his head at him and he is slung out of the pub and barred.

I then get the piss taken out of me for the rest of the night and the next day, saying that Peter Osgood had done me and I shit my pants! I got stick for weeks.

In 2002, a paperback book was published called *Scum Airways: Inside Football's Underground Economy*. It was written by Brighton University sociologist John Sugden, who had won the confidence of, and travelled around with, 'Big Tommy', a 6ft 4in, twenty-three stone sometime-tout from Manchester who ran a travel company taking fans to football matches. *Scum Airways* was a revealing insight into the workings of football's black economy of ticket scalpers, merchandise floggers, counterfeiters and grafters. Tony O'Neill made a couple of brief but sinister cameo appearances as 'Rocket O'Connor', a depiction he was deeply unhappy about. He saw it as an attempt by a rival to nobble his travel company by portraying it as the refuge of thugs and criminals. The book also came out at a sensitive time, when he was awaiting trial for violent disorder.

Big Tommy was in reality a well-known figure called Fat Tony.

TONY: We had never allowed Fat Tony to be part of the group since he had been seen in the Stretford cop shop by a certain person and the football intelligence officer, Bob Betts, came out with the words, 'Fucking hell Tony, what do you want now?' Fat Tony didn't see the kid sat there, but we got a report back. Then he later goes and sticks me in to a researcher about football violence and criminality who then wrote a book about it and tried to get my company wiped out. Draw your own conclusions.

I knew when I started the business that people would say I was a thug and would rip people off. That's why I didn't bother doing any advertising; it would only have brought it on top. The only way to really get people interested in your business is word of mouth. We don't have hooligans travelling with us; there's no such thing as hooligans now anyway. There are no mobs of thugs. Go and ask the football intelligence when was the last time they nicked a Cat C hooligan at Old Trafford for fighting. It has gone.

The players were showing their true colours as well. In August 2002 I did a trip to Budapest to watch United in a Champions League qualifying round against Zalaegerszeg. I do a trip there, no problems, people have had a good time and we are obviously expecting an easy win because we're playing a bunch of part-timers. Well, we all stood there and couldn't believe what we were watching. No-one expected to see such an inept perform-ance against a bunch of schoolteachers, mineworkers and bus drivers – and they scored near the end to win 1–0.

We weren't playing at their ground but at one of their rivals' grounds and at some point in the game it had gone off opposite where we stood against this other team's fans. People were running around. It didn't last long and got quelled by the police. But the game was a joke. There was no effort from any of the players.

Back at the airport everyone was gutted and I'm not happy, having arranged the trip. A few fans are singing, 'It's just like watching City.' They were loyal Reds; they weren't being abusive, they were taking the piss because that was the mood. The United players were going through Departures at the time and one kid where I'm stood says something to them. Next thing, David Beckham strides over as though he's the main man.

'Who are you?' he says to this kid. 'Call yourself a United fan?'

The kid didn't know what to say but I went straight over.

'Who the fuck do you think you are, you seventy grand a year, overpaid bastard? Fuck off before you get knocked out.'

He had a fucking cheek after that performance, having a go at someone who had paid money to follow the team. Beckham quickly sized up the situation, turned on his heels and scuttled off, followed by me hurling more abuse. There must have been a reporter around because the next day the story appeared in one of our cherished national tabloid rags.

We went on to beat them 5–0 at our place and Beckham scored a superb free kick, so perhaps I had an effect. In fact the second leg was over after twenty minutes – before a full house. Now, if we'd beaten them over there, no-one would have wanted to pay for the second leg. And what would ITV's viewing figures have been? Am I being cynical here or just clued-up?

Next thing up is my Crown Court case for the England game. I didn't deny being at the pub when it went off, but I strongly denied that my actions were violent. They claimed in court, without asking me the question in interview, that I deliberately went there with a gang for a fight. I know I never went there deliberately for a fight, because I had reasons to be there. The fact is, I wanted the landlord and bar staff as witnesses, because they would have been able to say what they saw, yet my solicitor was denied access to them.

Only when I was in jail did I learn the police had called the landlord into Bootle Street [police station] and asked him and several other landlords what had gone on in their pubs that day. The police have never declared this, they didn't even tell the Crown Prosecution Service, but I know it from another landlord who was interviewed at the same time. This is not me whingeing because I should have been banned from football a long time ago for what I'd done. I'm just letting people know what goes on.

Apart from verbal evidence, there was no surveillance or video footage of me, not even walking through Manchester city centre, probably the most high-density area of CCTV cameras in Britain. Yet the jury decided to find me guilty, on Friday the Thirteenth. I was then sentenced on 16 December 2002. I should have been sentenced on December 13, but the day before that I went to Birmingham to make a complaint about the police beating me up at Villa Park, because I had just been found not guilty of an offence there a week or two before. I make the complaint on the Thursday, I'm due to be sentenced the next day in Manchester Crown Court, then I get a phone call Friday morning telling me it has been put back until Monday. Now do we believe in coincidences or that the system is bent?

Because when I go to court on the Monday, I get sentenced to three years, nine months. There were no victims, I was the only one nicked, and to this day I am clueless as to why I got that sentence. Yet the circuit judge was going to give me *four* years, but couldn't because I had loads of good references.

I went straight to Strangeways. I was put on the top landing, G Wing, I have my kitbag, my clothes, all that paraphernalia. The screw takes me to the cell and there is a kid on the other side, a cleaner. I'm thinking, *here we go, just get your head down*. Then the kid shouts out, 'You've got a telly in your cell.' I immediately thought he was taking the piss, so I pointed at him and growled, 'Don't start taking the piss.' And he says, 'No, no, I'm telling you, you have got a telly in your cell.'

I go in the piss-stinking cell, because G Wing and K Wing are the pits – unless you happen to be a nonce – and there is a telly being watched by some silly car thief and I thought, *what is this?* It was a joke compared to when I had got five and a half years when I was twenty-one, when you got absolutely nothing, never opened your mouth and didn't answer back. These cunts were telling the screw to fuck off. Arrogant, the lot. That is the way life has gone.

I'm more and more baffled while I'm in that jail. You have got all your music systems, Play Stations. To me it is fucking mental. It creates chaos. The attitude is that no-one is bothered. Those doing short sentences aren't bothered because some of them have got more inside than they have got outside. So what is the fear of being locked up? You have no-one mithering you while you play your Play Station. I'm not into that but I like my relaxation and that is the first time in forty-odd years that I was able to relax. No pressure, nothing.

I'm in there twenty-one days and the next thing I'm in a Cat D jail in Sudbury, between Derby and Stoke. What a joke. Life of Riley. I was happy to be there. Feet up, telly, radio, not locked in, could wander around the grounds and the gardens. I was serving the screws food in the kitchen outside the jail. Fantastic. Just go back to my dorm with no screws anywhere, lie there and relax, read the papers, the phones are at the bottom. I wasn't a lover of the phones so I used the mobile.

One of the few stresses I got when I arrived there was finding myself a drink of brandy, because I didn't like whisky or vodka. So now and again we had a drink, a bottle of brandy between two or three of us. Who could argue? Saturday and Sunday lying in bed until 10:30 a.m., no rush. It was the most relaxing time of my life, with the occasional game of bowls played in the middle of the jail on a proper bowls pitch when it was nice and hot, which it was that summer.

Some City fans were in there who'd got three years. The first thing that comes out of their mouths is that it's my fault they received such long sentences, as I got three years nine months and the courts now think that's the norm. Yet these idiots had only filmed themselves attacking a pub full of Stockport, put the film on the Internet, then couldn't understand why they were arrested. They were the saddest twats I'd ever seen; they even wore clothes with 'City' written on. Maybe in the property office in Reception they had their inflatable bananas tucked away. Now I knew it was all over – these weren't thugs, they were people who lived sad lives bigging it up in the outside world by using technology.

Their case didn't stop others doing the same. It is very rare to see a mob of City after a game at Old Trafford, but while I was holed up in prison, the unbelievable happened; forty City, five minutes after the game, are at the top of Sir Matt Busby Way. They can't go left or forward, as there are lads hanging around waiting for a chance to get into them. The police are there so whoever goes first is definitely on a nicking. Well, one of the young lads runs straight up and whacks one, then the disorder starts.

Everyone now sees their chance and goes into them. City are having none of it and are running down Chester Road towards Altrincham with United trying to catch up. Not a chance. The only thing that caught up with them was two police horses going like the clappers and a police van and the only person nicked was the City lad who got slapped, as the police thought it was him who had caused it.

Yet while they were running down Chester Road, at least one of their number was filming with a handheld camcorder. It's bad enough getting nicked off CCTV but for one of the lads to film you, you've go to ask why they allow it. To go to jail but because one of your own side is filming evidence, that would take the biscuit. Just ask the City lads I met in jail how ill they were with it. It can't have helped that they met me, because I gave them proper stick.

Then one morning I got arrested, handcuffed, thrown in the back of a van with another prisoner and taken to Strangeways. I was banged up on K Wing for a couple of weeks with this other kid who had been brought back. I was accused of doing all sorts in the jail: drug running, beating people up, etc, but that did not happen. The kid banged up with me was only the one who stuck me in by putting notes in the box. But that is open jails for you: people get jealous and in a way it was a relief to be back in Strangeways. I kept myself to myself, got involved in nothing, did my jobs, got on with people, blanked people who needed to be blanked and just sat there. I carried on relaxing and passed the time away. All mod cons included.

The only stress I had was in the first two months and that was getting in touch with Debbie and telling her how to run the company and getting her and the kids over the shock. The kids did not know I was going to jail, so how do you explain that?

There were still fights to be had at the football but now they were few and far between.

JB: We played Birmingham City on a Tuesday night in February 2003 and went there firmed up, about eighty of us. Some had gone in cars, while I was on the train. Our biggest problem was not who we were going to fight but how we were going to dodge the police to get a fight. We stayed on at New Street, got off at a station on the way to West Brom and got in a boozer at midday. There was a good sixty of us in the boozer all day, no police, brilliant. We sent people out to get word and also to tell Birmingham where we were, but no show.

We set off for the game around 6:30. Just as we got to the ground, the police captured us. At the same time, this big Brummie kid, aged about twenty-five, stepped off the pavement and walked into our escort, up to Gary and me and said, 'You're United's firm, aren't you? If you want it, come out of your end after the game, turn right, keep going down, turn right again and you will find yourself on an estate.' Or words to that effect.

Most had tickets but I didn't. I ended up drinking in a hotel near the ground, so after the match I came back, waited by United's end and saw them come out. I found Gary and he said, 'Shall we do what the kid said?'

And thirty-five or forty of us did. We were walking near the Birmingham fans, against the flow, and we suddenly started to see people in Burberry. In other words, their firm. One of our lads says, 'These are them.' Then walks across and knocks one of them straight out.

Then we looked further down the road to this estate and

there they were. I reckon there was fifty of them and forty of us. They came towards us and we ran straight into them. Toe to toe, proper fighting. I got dropped – once again – but as I said to one of the lads afterwards when he took the piss about it, 'You don't get dropped if you are just a UN observer.' I got up, only to get hit again from the left and the right.

People were swarming around, fighting everywhere. It was dark and it was scary but we weren't going to back off. There was a copper with a video camera trying to film it but it was a free-for-all. It lasted maybe ten minutes but it was proper good. Then the sirens came and the vans and that was it, done. When we saw our hooligan coppers later they were fuming about it because they had no idea it had gone on.

I was a witness for a friend who got arrested and had to go back to Crown Court. The judge said to me, 'Were you fighting?'

'I was indeed,' I said.

I think he understood.

TONY: Bolton away in February 2003 saw the mobile phone come in handy. Now we have our man called Wing who is obsessed with football violence and talks all the time about it and this was one of his successes with the mobile phone, one of the few times it actually worked.

All day, Wing Commander is running about trying to avoid the police and get some of the lads to find the Bolton firm, but he was thwarted at all turns. Angry and frustrated, he was determined not to go home. So out comes his mobile and he gets hold of one of the Bolton lads. His mob have made their way by train away from Bolton but will be back, so he tells them to get their firm together and that he'll be back in two hours.

All the talking and organising can go pear-shaped at any moment as it takes only one copper to spot them, but their luck holds out. Now let this be a lesson to some of you hoolies who think that being in a large group makes you invincible. There were only thirty United. Wing even told Bolton which platform they were arriving at, and right on cue the lads piled off only to be confronted by up to 150 Bolton.

United's lads piled into them and one hell of a battle ensued. There were bottles, cans, bins, you name it, being used. This was pure, in-your-face violence. On the platform the battle was raging and United forced them back. The lads knew they were fighting for their lives. Eventually they forced Bolton over the bridge, where in the tight space some of the worst fighting went on.

United's lads kept going forward and were taking some stick but slowly forced them off the bridge. This was carnage as blood was everywhere but those who were injured just carried on. As Bolton retreated off the bridge it was the end for them as United charged again into them. Bolton lost the plot and started to run through the concourse and out into the street.

There were quite a few Bolton viciously twatted all over the station. Some United were also bloodied but it didn't matter at all. Bolton on that day thought they were going to smash our little firm and if they had done they would have all been screaming, 'We done United.' But there were only thirty Reds.

No bullshit, pure fact, so well done Wing and Co., another perfect day I missed through jail, life's a shit.

---

12 arrests as rival fans clash

A HUGE fight broke out between more than 150 rival football fans at Bolton railway station – leaving dozens of passengers terrified.

More than 100 Wanderers supporters are believed to have spilled out of nearby pubs to fight with a Manchester

United mob following the teams' 1–1 draw at the Reebok Stadium.

There were 12 arrests, including one for possession of an offensive weapon, following the battle and one man was taken to hospital with a head injury.

Rail staff cowered behind their counters and passengers looked on in terror as United fans got off a train from Manchester and charged across a walkway from the platform below.

They were met by a crowd of Wanderers fans and a brawl broke out.

The station was a scene of chaos following the fighting, with blood splattered across the floor and walls.

Scores of newspapers were taken from the stands of the station's newsagent and scattered across the ground. Phones were ripped from kiosks and fittings from the walls. Staff at the newsagents were too shocked to speak after the incident.

Dozens of police officers, who arrived on the scene within minutes, regained control at around 3.45 p.m. Afterwards, two fans with bruised and blooded faces were handcuffed by officers and held in a police van on Trinity Street.

Two elderly women alighting from trains at the station had to be helped through the debris by police.

One onlooker, who asked not to be named, said: 'The United fans came running out of the station as the Bolton fans came pouring in.

'They fought in the foyer and then back along the passage way. It was terrifying.'

Services from the station were cancelled as around 25 United fans were held on a train and police used hand-held video cameras in an attempt to identify those involved in the disturbances. Shopper Sue Littleton, aged 38, from Horwich, was unable to catch her train after arriving at the station following the violence.

She said: "What kind of animals behave like this? It is an absolute disgrace.

'I am so glad I wasn't here when it happened and feel terrible thinking about those who were. I didn't think things like this happened any more – how wrong I was.'

Bolton Evening News, 24 February 2003

JB: Bolton hate Man U, and it's a rough town. We arrive there, the train pulls up outside the Reebok, police everywhere. I said, 'I'm not getting off,' and Faz, Big James and a few other lads said the same.

This copper says, 'What are you doing?'

We said, 'We're not going to the match.'

He believed us, so the train goes through to Chorley and about eighteen of us get off and find a pub. We find a decent bar with Sky Sports, cushty, having a nice beer.

We decide we will get the train back and see what happens. The game finishes and there is now about thirty of us and we decide to get the train at about 5:30. Some guys were coming out of Chorley railway station. Bolton. We have a scuffle with them and they fuck off. I believe they were the guys who later returned and attacked United fans.

We get on this inter-city-style train. We are in the carriage and I hear someone on his mobile phone, a younger lad with us.

'Yeah, yeah, no problem.'

He said, 'It's Bolton. They said, "We're going to be waiting at Bolton station for you Munich cunts."'

So I told everyone to get in one carriage, because I had been down this road before, in London. I said, 'When the train pulls in, whoever is there, whatever is there, we are going to give it to them.'

The train comes into the station. I see all these lads going past the windows: Bolton. I open the carriage door and jump off while the train is still doing about five mph, see this big cunt is in front of me and I hit him with the momentum from the train and all the strength I can muster. At the same time the other doors have crashed open and the lads are off and into them. In about eight seconds it is done and dusted. From being there in a big mob with their fists up to do us, Bolton are blitzed. They were utterly taken by surprise when we came off fighting.

We then chase a few up the station bridge and banjo another one up there. We are all thinking, what a result, done them. Most of the United walk back down from the bridge but I'm still on it with another lad and we see about ten of them coming towards us. We run along the top of the bridge and shout, 'It's not over. Come on.'

I get this cunt good and put him down and my mate goes in and they are backing off. I get this cunt on the floor and his designer baseball hat has come off and I'm kicking him.

Someone says, 'JB, for fuck's sake, leave him, you're killing him.'

Then they all came over and we got to the bridge and the main concourse of the station was full of about 150 of them, all piling in. They charge at us. We ran into them and they were backing off but then they surged forward. We were strung across the entrance to the bridge like the Spartans. They wrecked the news stand and were throwing full cans of beer at us. Blood everywhere. And that genuinely lasted ten minutes on that bridge. If we backed off we were fucked. Well, we held it. But when I heard the sirens, I thought, *thank fuck*.

You could see the police behind them and now they were trying to get out. We legged back up the bridge, onto the platform and got on a two-carriage train to Manchester. Eventually the Old Bill turned up, looking at the blood and ripped shirts. They came on the train.

'Has anybody got any problems here?'

'No.'

'Anybody hurt?'

'No.'

'What happened?'

'Nothing. We just came on the platform and got attacked.'

'Is that it?'

'Yeah.'

What more could they do? I did a head count later and there were thirty-one of us. It was superb.

In October 2003, the European Champions League threw up one of those clashes that the fans relish and the football authorities dread: Manchester United versus Rangers. In the Seventies, these two teams had been the scourge of British football. Times had changed, but both were still both respected and feared in the unforgiving world of the soccer gangs. United were laying waste, while Rangers with their strong Loyalist links were friendly with the likes of Chelsea and still had a fearsome reputation.

JB: Rangers, we knew their history, supposed to be tasty, so the draw was manna from heaven for us and we were really up for it. It was a midweek game and most went up the night before; we stayed in the Hilton or somewhere. We met up with the Cockney firm and went into the town that night thinking it would be full of Rangers, but it was quiet. We were all setting out our stall for the next day, which we thought would be a proper biggie.

Some had had a recce and come back to the hotel and had actually phoned their pub, which is called The Doctors. It was in a big Loyalist area. The plan was to go in there when it opened, give them a welcome and see how they liked it. We arrived as the landlord was opening, in taxis. It was about ten minutes' walk from the ground, an area of old brownstone tenement flats. Opposite was a tenement block with a forty-foot Union Jack with 'Rangers' on it hanging outside. I think it was called Paisley Road West. No-one has ever been on that raid, in the heart of their territory; Celtic wouldn't dare.

The next morning we were there for opening time. The landlord was all right but gave us the odd quizzical look as he polished the beer glasses. After ten minutes he asked who we were supporting and when we told him he said, 'You do realise you're in a Rangers pub?'

'Don't give a fuck, mate,' was the reply.

He was still all right with us. First there was six of us, then ten, then twenty, with more arriving all the time, old lads from Bristol, Birmingham, London, turning up and greeting each other like long lost friends, just like in that *Football Factory* film, while the landlord was still polishing his glasses thinking, fuck me.

By 11.20 the pub was jammed and he was phoning for more staff. By 12.15 that pub was full, then the pub down the road filled and then we had four or five pubs down Paisley Road packed with United – and no police. Even at 1 p.m. there was no police or spotters. Rangers must have known we were there because people were riding round in taxis looking for them and telling lads who and where we were, and other people were getting texts from their firm. We thought it was only a matter of time before they turned up.

By 2 p.m. the odd Glasgow copper had turned up and had a look in the pub. By about 4 p.m. people wanted to fight. They had been there since 11 a.m. and had had enough. We knew the police were going to come and capture us, so we had to make our move. There was 400 lads, minimum, everyone having got there by different means. I wanted it, that was what I had come for. It was about doing them on their own manor.

It got to about twenty to five and that was it: we came out of The Doctors, the main heads, and everyone else clocks it. Two mounted police outside the pub were flapping because as we moved, all the others moved too, all jumping up and suddenly you have this massive firm of lads, not a scarf or badge in sight, and they started to get a bit heavy-handed and pulled out the long truncheons and shouted, 'Get back, you bastards.'

'Get fucked, you Scottish cunt.'

Then we broke into a bit of a canter, with the police trying to keep everybody back. There was a lot of shouting and screaming but the police had no control. They were getting pushed out of the way and we went down this big long road looking for Rangers.

We came to a bar on the left with lots of Rangers in it, staring out of the windows, but the doors were locked and they wouldn't come out. We kept coming to bars and they were behind the doors. There was a little Tube station or shopping centre with an escalator and about twenty of them burst out of there and they got absolutely smashed back down, and that was the only surge of resistance we got pre-game. This went on all the way to the ground, just duelling with the police. For Rangers it was a big, big embarrassment.

I didn't go in the game and we had quite a few running battles, about twenty-five of us, during the game with pockets of them. Two or three United fans were slashed outside because Rangers were resorting to hitting and running.

The night before, we were with Wing and he had met some Rangers heads in their forties who ran a lap dancing club and fifteen of us went down there for an hour or two. We saw them after the game in the town centre when seventy of us went into a wine bar. They were supposed to be connected to organised crime and were driving around in a four-by-four Land Rover and kept cruising by the bar. One lad came in and wanted to speak to Gary.

'We should have turned out,' he said. 'We are embarrassed. There's sixty of us now in this pub a couple of streets away if you want it.'

Basically we told them to fuck off. We had our police spotters with us and we said, 'If you want it now, mate, you have got to come and get us. Never mind being in the pub down the road. We're here, we've been here all day and it's up to you.' He was devastated. Then he gave it the verbals about them bringing 200 top lads to the return at Old Trafford.

One of the Glasgow newspapers later called us 'masked men in black'. That was the best United mob since the days when we used to go to Chorlton Street for the coaches to Chelsea in the mid-Eighties.

UP TO 50 English soccer hooligans were arrested last night as violence broke out before the Battle of Britain clash.

Fights erupted along roads leading to Ibrox – where Rangers met Manchester Utd – with baton-wielding cops pouncing on the brawling yobs.

It is understood thugs intent on causing trouble had travelled to Glasgow – despite having no tickets for the glamour Champions League match.

Witnesses told how groups of casuals were picking fights

with BOTH Rangers and Man Utd fans as they headed for Ibrox.

James Totten, 27, of Glasgow, said: 'The atmosphere on the main road was extremely tense. I saw this one guy knock about three people down for no reason.

'The police quickly wrestled him to the ground and put him in the back of a van.

'I saw a similar incident happen about four times within about 10 minutes while walking to Ibrox.

'I had my son with me and was very worried about his safety – but luckily the police were excellent.'

Police said there were 50 arrests before and during the game. Twenty-five of the arrests were made during violence on Paisley Road West – the main route leading to Rangers' stadium – before the match, a source added.

Gangs of thugs congregated in backstreet bars ahead of the crunch match, which Rangers lost 1–0.

In one sinister incident, a coach dropped off more than 100 men dressed head-to-toe in black at the tiny Stanley Bar – just a mile from Ibrox. But within minutes a huge police presence arrived to move them on.

A barmaid from the pub said: 'It was really weird because suddenly this massive group of men came in.

'None of them had football strips on and they were all dressed in black. They didn't have Manchester accents either – they were more southern than that.

'But suddenly police vans and cops on horseback showed up and moved them on. It was all very strange.'

Furious Gers fans claimed they couldn't get into diehard Rangers pubs – because they were packed with United supporters.

Some posted messages on the club's unofficial website followfollow.com.

One wrote: 'There are police on the doors in every bar. It looks like it could all turn very nasty as Rangers fans can't get into their own bars.'

More than 7,000 Manchester Utd fans travelled north for the tie.

Only 2,500 had briefs for the match – with others hoping they could land surplus tickets on the black market.

But they were left to wander the streets after failing to get their hands on ANY spare tickets.

Extra uniformed police were drafted in to control roaming crowds – and plain-clothed officers were placed undercover to pick out hooligans. Most city bars hired extra security in case trouble flared.

More than 500 United fans packed into the Arches bar in Glasgow City centre, which was booked especially by the travelling support.

The Sun, 24 October 2003

SALFORD VIKING: Opposite The Doctors was a pub called the Grapes and they had a massive Loyalist banner outside it. Some of our young 'uns tried to rip it down and the Rangers had to drag the banner in and shut the doors. We came out of the Doctors, about thirty of us, and bumped into a group of Rangers fans from Northern Ireland. You can't drink beer on the streets of Glasgow but all of this coachload got off with bottles and the coppers turned a blind eye. That told us these guys were UVF or LVF, one of those groups. The next thing, the shout goes up and we blitz them.

Ricky Jones was arrested and held overnight along with some of these Irish blokes. One of them said to him, 'We're the UVF.' Ricky replied, 'Well, we're the pissheads from Salford.'

In court the next day they basically respected us and said,

'No-one has ever come to Glasgow and done that. Not even Celtic have ever tried to do that.'

It was brilliant turnout, a throwback to the Seventies. It would equate to the firm that once marched from Stratford to West Ham, but twenty years older, wiser – and dafter.

The return game was touted in the media as the 'Battle of Britain', with 10,000 Rangers fans expected and dire predictions of football hooligans from all over the country turning up to join in the expected punchfest. In the event a huge police operation and the apparent no-show of Rangers' ICF as a force meant the evening passed relatively peacefully.

JB: So what happened? A small firm of them turned up near City's ground, about thirty, drinking with City, who they know, but they didn't turn up at Old Trafford. I heard a dozen showed at the Trafford Hall pub and got smashed.

Others were ready to have a pop at us when the numbers were in their favour. A couple of seasons ago we played Wolves. Most of our lads stayed in the ground but about fifteen stayed outside and went in a city centre bar. I was with a few lads from Royton. There was Wolves in there and they half knew we were United but they weren't sure. A few more Wolves came in and eventually this skinhead walked up and said, 'Where are you from?'

'Oldham, why?'

Brain of Britain couldn't understand this. 'Fuck off,' he said. 'You are not just coming in here. Fuck off out or you are going to get hurt.'

The pub started to fill up then and I told the lads we would have to leave in twos or we would never get out. We started to filter out, being watched by the Wolves, who couldn't really weigh up what was happening.

I was shitting it but I was the last one to leave. I had to play it cool. I came out on the street and our lot were getting in taxis. There was a pub opposite and fifty or sixty suddenly piled out and they were boys, probably banned from the ground. It was quite scary but in the end we got out without getting done in.

Villa away was a triumph though. After that game we got on a train at that little station that takes you from Villa Park to New Street. Our police had us but we got off at Birmingham and fucked off into the town centre and eventually our hoolie cops went home. Someone said Villa were in their main pub. We go and they are all there in the doorway. We run at the pub, knock fuck out of these cunts on the door, run in and chase them across the pub, chairs being thrown and the windows going. It went on for ages. There was about thirty of them in there and they were shocked because we just came right in. As we left people were throwing dustbins. Then we went straight back to the station and were on the train before the cops knew where we were.

The hooligan coppers called us 'crafty cunts' the next time we saw them. But for the past four or five years the police have been swamping us, compared to any other club. They have said, 'Wherever this lot go, there will be trouble.'

TONY: Other clubs now have their Men in Black too. Everton are one that have caught up with the fashion. They also claimed a bit of a result against United in February 2005 after a game at Goodison. The truth is a group of thirty United had just come out of the ground and were making their way back to the train station with a police escort. The main lot of United have all been herded together in a bigger escort further back, but this thirty have been allowed to continue, with football intelligence officers in attendance. Which seems strange. The main mob of United and straight members are 300 yards behind. People don't understand why the FI officers and Liverpool police didn't tell this thirty to wait.

When they came to the Valley, Everton had all gathered there. The police have actually walked the United into this situation. Everton all came out and United stood their ground. It ended up a big heap on the floor. United were giving as good as they got against 150–200 Everton. They stood and took it. I would like to see that reversed down some street in Manchester. The lads were forced to give and take whacks but no-one was badly hurt. Everton claim they battered United, but they didn't, even at odds of five or six to one.

The fight was filmed and led to the usual raids afterwards, but the police need to answer why they led that United group down towards a big group of Everton. If they were football intelligence, surely they knew what would happen?

Chapter Fifteen

THE FINAL WHISTLE

IN 2005, IT was revealed that Greater Manchester Police had issued more football banning orders the previous season than any force outside London: a total of 272 orders for the eight league clubs in the county. Despite this sobering statistic, organised hooliganism at the biggest club, Manchester United, was all but dead. With Tony O'Neill banned, and other potential leaders either abroad or no longer interested, it finally appeared that the days of the all-conquering Red Army were finally over.

TONY: I came out of prison in the summer of 2004 and was on a tag for four and a half months. I had to be in the house between 7 p.m. and 8 a.m. It wasn't a problem; I was usually in by 5 p.m. anyway and there was no point going out after that. My daily routine was basically doing what I had done in jail, sitting at home with my feet up reading the papers. I was also banned from attending any football matches.

I finished writing my first book, which I had started in prison, and about ten days before it was due to be published, my tag finished. So on the Saturday, my first night out in years, I met up with a few lads to have a booze. It wasn't planned, just a drink with friends. As it happens, a few more turn up, a few women in our company, then we move on somewhere else. We don't go to town in case of trouble, and I end up in Chorlton in south Manchester. I am still on licence and can go back to prison for another two years if I breach it, so I am certainly not interested in any trouble, and the people I was with weren't out for any bother.

As it happened, only a few of us made it to Chorlton. We went in a pub and I was having a good time. Unbeknown to me, something has happened and the next thing I know it has gone off. There is a mass brawl. Somewhere along the line, someone has come in with a gun and it has gone off. Here we go again. A single bullet has gone through me and out of my back, piercing my liver and lung and severing nerves.

I went down on the floor in a pool of blood. Out. People were saying I had gone, I was dead, but my pal Harry was having none of it. Luckily the ambulance was there almost immediately, and the doctors at Manchester Royal Infirmary saved my life. I'm one lucky man to be alive. I remember nothing about it, it is a total blank. I can't even remember anything about being taken to the hospital. Though I do know that apart from the fact that I was shot, and had been banned from every soccer ground, *The Sun* newspaper got almost everything wrong when they reported it – including the spelling of my name. Bastards.

———————

'WORST SOCCER THUG' GUNNED DOWN IN PUB

Britain's worst soccer yob has been gunned down in a gang feud.

Tony O'Neil, 46, was shot in the stomach in a packed pub on Saturday night.

Last night he was in intensive care under police guard after emergency surgery for a gunshot wound.

Convicted thug O'Neil is said to have waded into an argument between rival gangsters in a Manchester pub.

A pal said: 'There was a row going on in the pub between some of Tony's friends and another group. He sorted out the other group, who left the pub. But one of them came back with a gun and shot Tony in the stomach before running off.

'At first it looked like Tony was going to die.'

Manchester United fan O'Neil, of Cheadle, was jailed for hooliganism and boasts of being the world's biggest thug.

He is currently banned from every soccer ground in Britain.

Police are quizzing two men and a woman over the shooting.

The Sun, 16.11.04

It was two days later that I came round and was able to open my eyes. I couldn't speak, and was full of tubes. I had more tubes than a map of London. But one of my first comments was, 'Not to worry, forget it, I'm alive it doesn't matter.' That's my motto anyway. Same as on the football terraces or fighting in the streets: if you get knocked down, just get back up and carry on, because whatever happens, happens.

I have damaged nerves, can't lift things, can't twist. They brought me out after four days from the High Dependency Unit. I don't know anyone else who had ever been released from there that quickly; I should have been kept on the ward for two weeks to monitor my organs but they sent me home. I lay down at home with this nerve damage and every time I moved my neck, my arm, it was agony. There is nothing worse than nerve pain. Imagine shoving a needle into the nerve endings in your teeth – that's what it was like with every movement.

I ended up back in the hospital. I was in a real bad way but the doctor wouldn't come out to see me, so I told my wife Debbie that if I got any worse to take me to casualty. I couldn't even get off the settee. The next day the nurse came round to take staples out of my body. She realised I was in a bad way, got the woman doctor from around the corner and half an hour later the ambulance arrived to take me back to the MRI. I was bleeding internally – but when I got to the hospital, they couldn't find my notes. For six and a half hours I'm in a cubicle being pumped full of morphine to stop the pain. They didn't find my records until the day after. Nothing bothered me more than going back to the Royal Infirmary, and the non-existent after-care.

I got released early December 2004 and have been in a state pretty much right up to this day. I was sent on my way with a concoction of morphine tablets, gabapentin and some other tablets. Gabapentin has horrendous side effects, yet I was never advised about it. I was that doped out of my head I was taking thirteen morphine tablets a day. I didn't have a clue where I was for three months. I was smashed out of my skull until March 11, when I walked into an acupuncturist in Stretford and it was the best thing I have ever done. I realised that of all the times I have been in hospital, I've never once seen a Chinese person.

I had decided football was over before I got nicked. I should never have gone in town the day I was arrested, regardless. I had already had enough. But I put myself in a position and it went pear-shaped. In many ways I think the trip to Rangers when I was inside was our testimonial, the last big day out. I will always be a United fan and will always follow them, but in a different way.

* * *

The trouble is over. I will always have lots of fantastic friends there because at the end of the day Man U is one thing: a family.

And everyone else hates us.

STEVE BARNES: Though I'm no longer in the police force, I go to games and look at the areas they normally met and there doesn't seem to be a group of them. I have chatted to Tony and he's a very influential character and seems to know everybody. He was the focal point for it all. Whenever he was there, he was the leader and when he said the word they would go. He had that influence and because he is not on the scene, it has gone. But whenever people say hooliganism has gone, I am wary. It doesn't take much to start it up again. If the police were to relax, it only takes a new group to come along.